Home Ground

A Geography of Northern Ireland

Derek Polley

Colourpoint

© Derek Polley 1999

ISBN 0 898392 54 4

8 7 6 5 4 3 2 1

Layout and design: Colourpoint Books
Cover design: Barry Craig at Colourpoint
Printed by: ColourBooks

All rights reserved. No part of this publication may be reproduced or transmitted in any form or by any means, electronic, mechanical, photocopying, recording or otherwise, without the prior written permission of the publisher.

In general, throughout the book, the name Derry is used when referring to the city. The county is referred to as Londonderry.

Colourpoint Books
Unit D5 Ards Business Centre
Jubilee Road
NEWTOWNARDS
Co Down
BT23 4YH

Tel: 01247 820505
Fax: 01247 821900
info@colourpoint.co.uk
www.colourpoint.co.uk

Derek Polley, MEd, BA, Dip Ed, DASE, is Head of Geography at Comber High School. He graduated with a BA from Queen's University, Belfast, in 1969 and added a Diploma in Education in 1970. He taught for two years in Sierra Leone. He has also taught in Ballynahinch High, Movilla High and Knockbreda High before being appointed to Comber in 1991. This has given him wide experience of teaching Geography to the Junior School and also at CSE, 'O' level, GCSE and 'A' level.

Picture credits
Cover: © ESA 1998 M-SAT 01494 440567
Page 8: Reproduced from the 1979 Ordnance Survey 1:50 000 map with the permission of the Controller of Her Majesty's Stationery Office, © Crown Copyright, Permit number 1327

All photographs by the author except the following:
Bill Polley 11; 13 (1); 19 (chalk, basalt, White Rocks, Giant's Causeway); 26 (H and I); 28 (M); 29 (O and P); 77 (top).
Fermanagh District Council 19 (Marble Arch Caves); 22 (Marble Arch Caves).
Tony Stone Images 31 (poor visibility).
Seagate 69.
Tayto 72, 73.
Montupet 70.
Malcolm Johnston 30 (4 and 5).
Norman Johnston 43, 44, 47, 49, 51 (1, 3, 4).
Grateful thanks to Ulster Television for the photograph of Mr Frank Mitchell on page 31.

Contents

Mapwork 4

Ecosystems 13

Physical geography 18

Weather. 30

Settlement. 42

Population 54

Economic activity 64

Using the Internet. 78

Glossary and index 79

Author's Note

This book would not have been possible without the help and support of the following people. Aileen Corbett (Glastry College), Bill Polley (Carrickfergus Grammar), Ken Sittlington (Movilla High) and Martin Thom (Sullivan Upper School), their colleagues and pupils who reviewed and improved on each chapter. Richard Watson at Marble Arch Caves and the staff at the Enniskillen Tourist Information Centre helped with photographs and information in Chapter 3. Rob Hoare at www.worldclimate.com gave permission to use the climate statistics in Chapter 4. David Polley's A Level Case Study formed the basis of page 47. Bob Brown (Tayto), Harry Gray (Montupet), Ian O'Leary (Seagate), Mark Wilson (Enkeymore Farm), and Paul Stevenson (Stevenson Quarries) all arranged a visit to their premises, took time out of their busy schedules and put up with my endless questions with patience and good humour. They gave me far more information than I could ever use. Dorothy Beattie, Martina McIlvenna and Pauline Wylie at Shandwick provided the information on Sainsbury's. Gerry Camplisson, Kristine Gillespie and Jean Barklie at the NITB provided the information on tourism on pages 76 and 77. Dr Bill MacAfee at the University of Ulster was the source of most of the information on the Internet, and gave helpful advice on layout. Thanks also to Isabel Hood at the F H Ebbitt Field Centre at Bryansford for the use of their weather instruments in Chapter 4. Thanks are also due to all the staff at Colourpoint who gave me the chance to write the book which has been screaming to get out for the last twenty years.

Finally to my long-suffering wife Tanya, who has put up with this book for the last eight months, thanks for the help and support.

Derek Polley, August 1999

Links to all websites mentioned in this book can be found at www.colourpoint.co.uk/Educational/homeground.html

Mapwork

Maps are sometimes called the tool of the geographer. If you are going to study geography you will need to be able to use different types of maps. These will vary from a map of your school to a map of the world. A book of maps is called an *atlas* and usually gives world maps, continent maps and country maps. These are all drawn to different scales. In this section you will find three maps not found in most atlases – a map of Northern Ireland, a map of Ireland and a 1:50000 Ordnance Survey map of part of Northern Ireland. Most maps have a frame and use colour to make them easier to understand, but they should all have a title, key, scale and a north point.

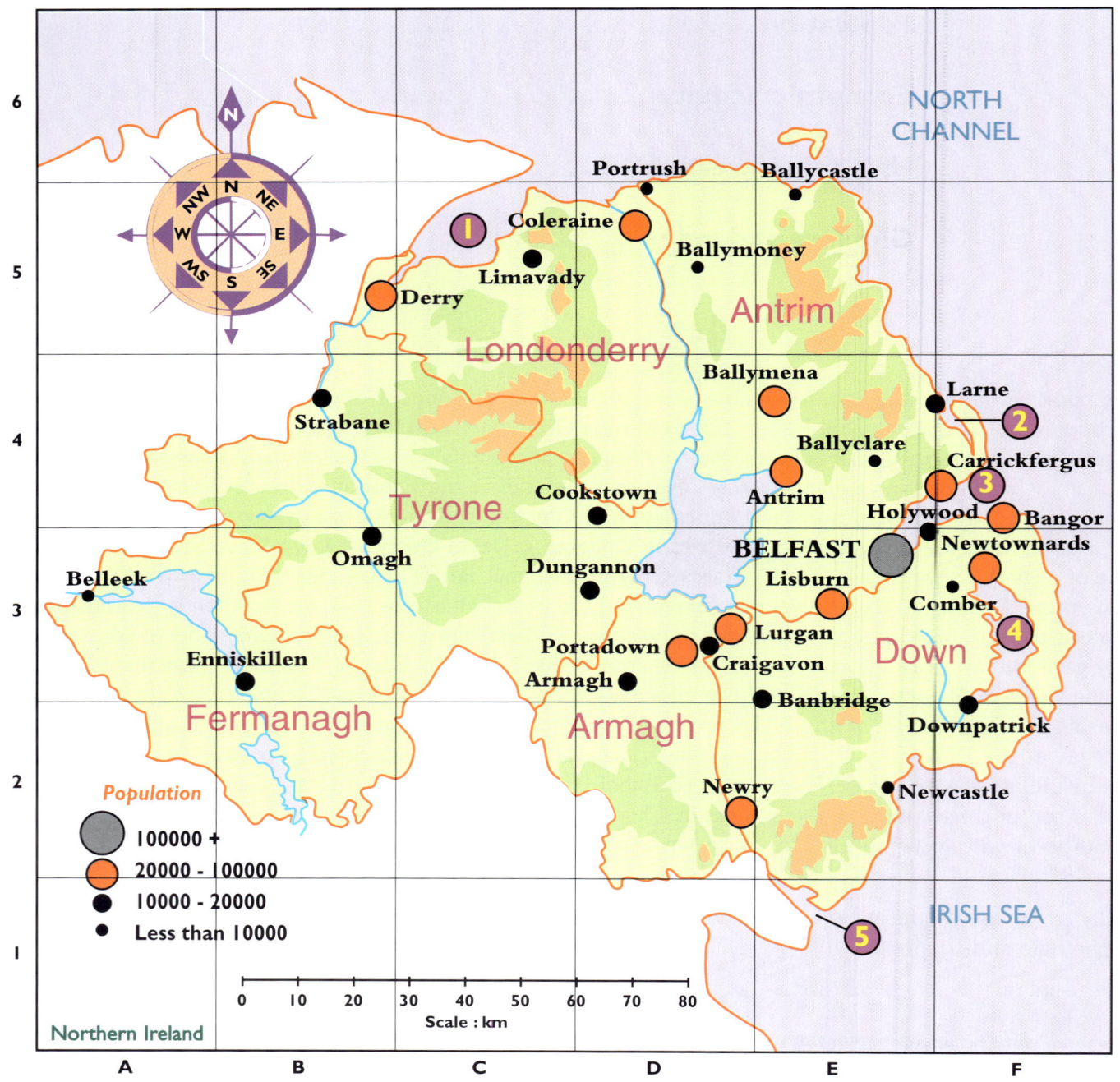

Population
- 100000 +
- 20000 - 100000
- 10000 - 20000
- Less than 10000

Northern Ireland

Exercises

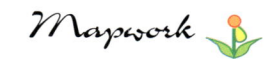

Northern Ireland is part of the United Kingdom (see page 55). It consists of six counties that can be remembered by the acronym FATLAD or FATDAD. Use the maps of Northern Ireland on pages 4 and 23, and/or your atlas to answer the following questions.

1. Name the six counties that make up Northern Ireland.
2. Name the three large freshwater loughs in Northern Ireland.
3. Name the sea area east of Northern Ireland.
4. Name the island off the north coast.
5. There are five sea loughs or inlets numbered on the map. Can you say what they are?

Direction

Give the following directions using the eight-point compass:

From	To
Belfast	Newry
Omagh	Portrush
Antrim	Ballycastle
Derry	Portadown
Larne	Comber
Ballymena	Dungannon

Distance

Copy and complete the following table by working out the straight-line distance between the points, saying in which direction you would be going. Use the linear scale on the map.

From	To	Distance	Direction
Larne	Antrim	??	??
Portadown	Armagh	??	??
Bangor	Newtownards	??	??
Limavady	Coleraine	??	??
Omagh	Strabane	??	??
Enniskillen	Belleek	??	??

Extension work

1. Which county does not border Lough Neagh?
2. Which county is the smallest?
3. Belfast is spread over two counties; name them both.
4. Name the three counties that do not have a coastline.
5. Name all the towns within 30km of Belfast.
6. Name four seaside holiday resorts.
7. Name three towns in County Londonderry.
8. If people talk about "The North West", what county do they mean?
9. If people talk about "West of the Bann", what counties do they mean?
10. Which two counties face east towards England and Scotland?

Mapwork

Map of Ireland

Exercises

Ireland is part of the British Isles (see page 54). It is divided in two parts by an international border. Northern Ireland is part of the United Kingdom which is made up of Great Britain (England, Scotland and Wales) and Northern Ireland. The Republic of Ireland is an independent state with Dublin as its capital. Before 1922, all of the island of Ireland was part of the United Kingdom. In that year the island was divided into the two parts we see on the map. The Republic of Ireland has different names. It is sometimes called Éire, the Irish Republic or just Ireland. Look at the map of Ireland and answer the following questions:

1 Name the four provinces of Ireland.
2 How many counties are there in each province?
3 Which three counties of Ulster are not in Northern Ireland?
4 Name the largest city in Munster.

Direction

1 Which county is west of Sligo?
2 Which county is north of Kilkenny?
3 Which province is in the south east corner of Ireland?
4 Which county is furthest north?
5 Which county is furthest south?
6 Which county is furthest east?
7 Which county is furthest west?
8 Which direction is Cork from Dublin?

Distance

Copy and complete the following table by working out the distance between the points, saying in which direction you would be going. Use the linear scale on the map.

From	To	Distance	Direction
Dublin	Dundalk	??	??
Dundalk	Belfast	??	??
Dublin	Belfast (add the first two answers!)	??	??
Cork	Dublin	??	??
Cork	Belfast (add the last two answers!)	??	??

Copy and complete the following paragraph, which is about the size of Ireland.

Ireland is not a large country. It measures ..... km from Ballycastle in the north to Bantry in the south. From Clifden in the west to Dublin in the east is only ..... km. Dublin and Belfast, the two capital cities, are ..... km apart.

Extension Work

1 Name the six counties of Munster.
2 Name two towns in County Wexford.
3 Name the counties which surround County Offaly.
4 Name the seas to the east, south and west of Ireland.

Use your atlas to answer the following:
1 Larne, Dun Laoghaire, Cork, Rosslare and Belfast are ferry ports. Find out where in the UK and/or Europe the ferries sail to.
2 What is the largest town in Connaught?
3 What country would you reach if you sailed south from Cork?
4 Name the large lake between Counties Clare and Tipperary.
5 Name the large lake between Counties Westmeath and Roscommon.

Giant's Causeway
Port na Tober
Port na Spaniagh
Girona wreck site
The Amphitheatre
Hamilton's Seat
Plaiskin Head
Plaiskin Farm
Portmoon House
Portnabrock
Contham Head
Hawks Hollow
The Organ
Grand Causeway
Port Ganny
Great Stookan
Giant's Chair
CROYER HILL
Port Moor
Portnagovna
Geeragh Point
Dunseverick Castle
Feigh Upper
Feigh Lower
Milltown
Dunshammer
Tonduff
B146
Carrowreagh Bridge
Portnaboe
Leckilroy Cove
The Mile Stone
Runkerry Point
Pollrinck
The Ladle
Runkerry House
Salmon Fishery
Cave
Hotel
Causeway Head
Souterrain
Aird
Lisserluss
Waterfall
Carrowreagh
Feigh Bridge
Artimacormick
Carnside
Ballymoy
Carncolp
School
Crannoge
Newbuildings
Craig
Ballylinny
Lisnagunogue Lower
Garage
Lisbellanagroagh Beg
Rath
Bushfoot Strand
Salmon Fishery
Glashan Isle
Seagull Rock
Leckboy
Seaport Lodge
Dunes
Dooey
The Fingers
A2
Carnkirk
Ballyallaght
Quarry (dis)
Lisnagunogue Upper
Lisbellanagroagh More
CH
Bushfoot
Earthworks
Kilcoobin
Castlenagree
Lisnagunogue Upper
Drumnagessan House
B145
PORTBALLINTRAE
Ballytaylor
Dundarave
Islandoo
Coolnagorr
Boneyclassagh
MP
Gortnacapple
School
BUSHMILLS
Distillery
Clogher South
Radio Station
Islandcorr
Araboy
ROUND HILL
Montalto
Craigaboney
B17
Garage
Eagry
Eagry Bridge
Carnanreagh
Turfahun
Ballyleckan
Ballyness
MS
Garage
Walk Mill
Bush River
Ballyness
Ballyhemlin
Turfahun
Islands of Carnmoon
Magherintendry
Ballytober
Curramoney
The Haw
Craig Park
School
Standing Stone
Ballylough
Billy
Rectory
Drumyaran Bridge
Drumyaran
Whitegate
Townend
Knocknadrook
The Traill Crest
Cabragh
Whinhill
Ballyloughbeg
Cozies
Ballylough House
Castlecat
School
Straidbilly
Revallagh North
Ballyclogh (Centre)
B66
Loughlynch
Liscolman
Revallagh South
Sch
Cloonty
Risk
Ballyrock North
Seneirl
Ballydivity
The Island
Carnbore
Seneirl Bridge
Island Carragh South
Ballywatt East
Old Town
Rockland Crescent
Islandrose
Keel
Ballyrock South
Ballyhunsley
The Springs
Kilmoyle
Ballyrock Irish
Ballynarry Upper
Islandahoe
Toberdoney
Carnglass Beg
Ballyhibistock
Coole
Toberdoney Cross Roads
Deffrick Bridge
B67
Lisnisk
Deepstown
Manse
Rath
Sch
Derrykeighan
Five Acres
Ballymacfin
Kilmahamogue

1 : 50 000

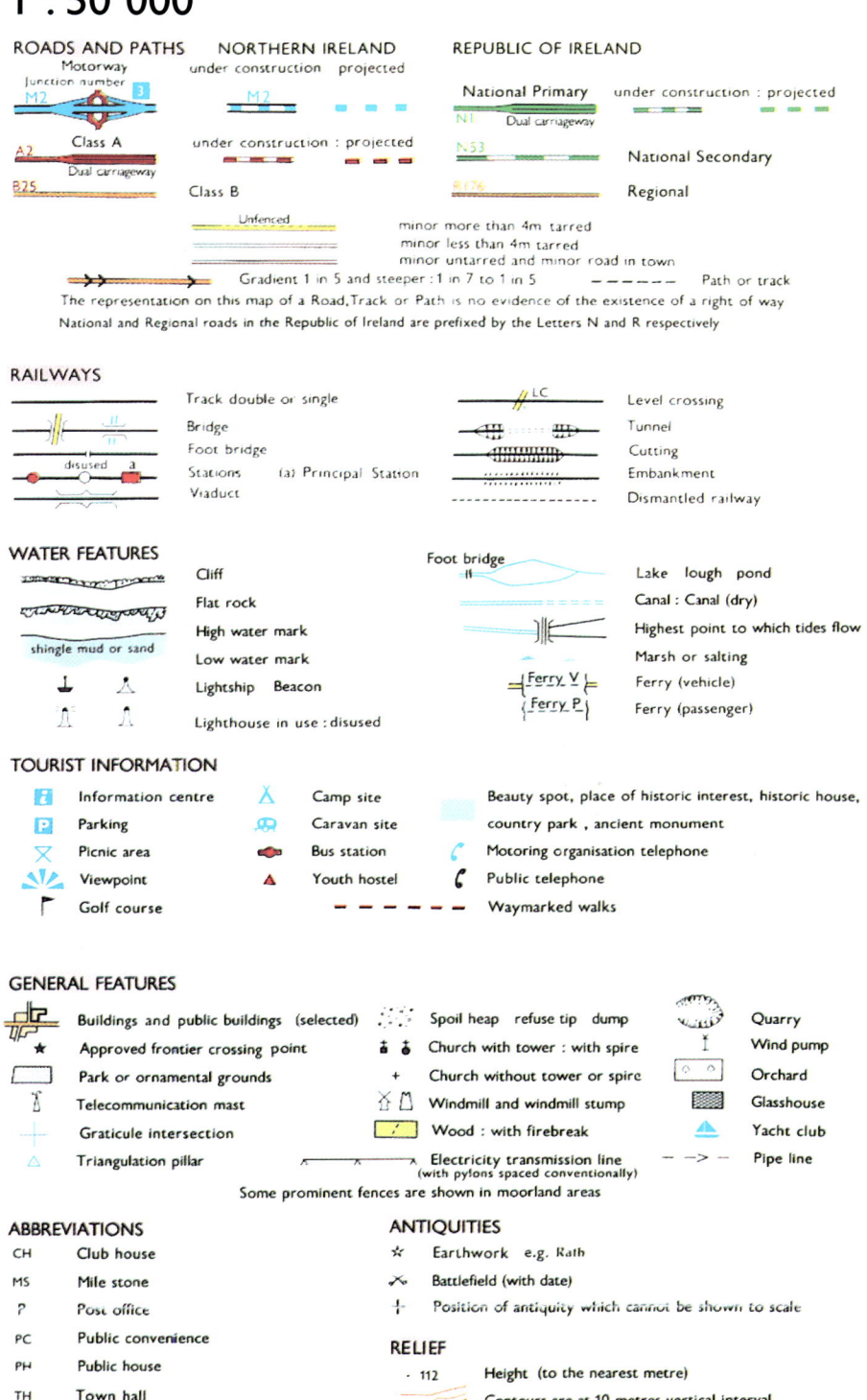

ROADS AND PATHS

NORTHERN IRELAND
- Motorway (Junction number) — M2 ... 3
- under construction ; projected — M2
- Class A — A2
- Dual carriageway
- under construction : projected
- Class B — B25

REPUBLIC OF IRELAND
- National Primary — N1
- under construction : projected
- Dual carriageway
- National Secondary — N53
- Regional — R178

- Unfenced
- minor more than 4m tarred
- minor less than 4m tarred
- minor untarred and minor road in town
- Gradient 1 in 5 and steeper : 1 in 7 to 1 in 5
- Path or track

The representation on this map of a Road, Track or Path is no evidence of the existence of a right of way

National and Regional roads in the Republic of Ireland are prefixed by the Letters N and R respectively

RAILWAYS

- Track double or single
- Bridge
- Foot bridge
- Stations   (a) Principal Station
- Viaduct
- Level crossing — LC
- Tunnel
- Cutting
- Embankment
- Dismantled railway
- disused

WATER FEATURES

- Cliff
- Flat rock
- High water mark
- Low water mark
- shingle mud or sand
- Lightship   Beacon
- Lighthouse in use : disused
- Foot bridge
- Lake lough pond
- Canal : Canal (dry)
- Highest point to which tides flow
- Marsh or salting
- Ferry V — Ferry (vehicle)
- Ferry P — Ferry (passenger)

TOURIST INFORMATION

- Information centre
- Parking
- Picnic area
- Viewpoint
- Golf course
- Camp site
- Caravan site
- Bus station
- Youth hostel
- Beauty spot, place of historic interest, historic house, country park, ancient monument
- Motoring organisation telephone
- Public telephone
- Waymarked walks

GENERAL FEATURES

- Buildings and public buildings (selected)
- Approved frontier crossing point
- Park or ornamental grounds
- Telecommunication mast
- Graticule intersection
- Triangulation pillar
- Spoil heap refuse tip dump
- Church with tower : with spire
- Church without tower or spire
- Windmill and windmill stump
- Wood : with firebreak
- Electricity transmission line (with pylons spaced conventionally)
- Quarry
- Wind pump
- Orchard
- Glasshouse
- Yacht club
- Pipe line

Some prominent fences are shown in moorland areas

ABBREVIATIONS

CH	Club house
MS	Mile stone
P	Post office
PC	Public convenience
PH	Public house
TH	Town hall

ANTIQUITIES

- Earthwork e.g. Rath
- Battlefield (with date)
- Position of antiquity which cannot be shown to scale

RELIEF

- ·112 Height (to the nearest metre)
- 50 Contours are at 10 metres vertical interval

Altitudes are given in metres above Mean Sea Level at Malin Head, Co Donegal

NORTH POINTS

Magnetic north was 8° 15' (147 mils) west of grid north at the centre of the map in 1989

Annual change which is not constant, is about 10° (3mils) east

True north is 1° 19' (24 mils) west of grid north at the centre of the map

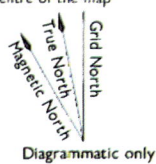

True North / Grid North / Magnetic North

Diagrammatic only

BOUNDARIES

- International Boundary
- County Boundary
- L G D Boundary
- County & L G D Boundary
- National Forest Park
- Forest Recreational Area
- NT — National Trust always open
- NT — National Trust opening restricted

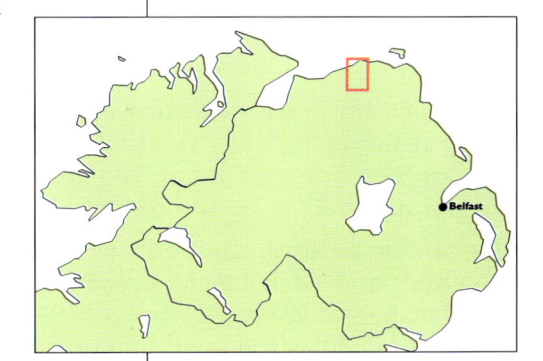

COMPILATION NOTES

Compiled from photographically reduced 1:10 000 Irish Grid material

Mapwork Exercises

Study the OS map of the Bushmills area on page 8 and use it to answer the following questions.

Four figure grid references
Say whether each statement is true or false:

1 There is a school in square 9238.
2 The River Bush flows through square 9335.
3 There is a rath in square 9641.
4 Square 9243 is mostly land.
5 Bushmills is in square 9440.
6 There is a church with a spire in square 9538.

Six figure grid references

Give a reference for the following:

1 Portballintrae Caravan Site
2 Bushmills Tourist Information Centre
3 Derrykeighan School
4 The public telephone in Castlecat
4 The Girona wreck site

Say what is found at each reference:

(a) 943361
(b) 936425
(c) 962438
(d) 963450
(e) 966454

Direction
Give the following directions using the eight-point compass:

From		To		Direction
1 Bushmills	9440	Deffrick bridge	9834	??
2 Derrykeighan	9633	Billy	9538	??
3 Ballyallaght	9642	Bushmills	9440	??
4 Caravan site	9241	Giant's Causeway	9444	??
5 Lisnagunogue Lower	9742	Rath	9333	??

Direction, distance and scale
This is a 1:50000 map, which means that 1cm on the map represents 50000 cm on the land which is 500m or half a kilometre. It is easier to say 2cm represents 1km. This makes measuring easy. You simply measure the distance in cm using your ruler then divide your answer by two. Copy and complete the following table by working out the straight-line distance between the points, saying in which direction you would be going:

From		To		Distance	Direction
1 Carnside Farm	(949435)	Car Park	(946439)	??	??
2 Carrowreagh Bridge	(972444)	Golf Course	(936425)	??	??
3 Church with tower	(939405)	Standing stone	(934383)	??	??
4 Lisnagunogue Church	(979430)	56 metre spot height	(952404)	??	??
5 Clubhouse	(934423)	Souterrain	(951439)	??	??

Height
There are three ways of showing height on the map:
i) Spot height eg 46m at 949383.
ii) Contour line eg 90m at 963450.
iii) Colour shading eg the darker the colour the higher the land.

Use any or all of these methods to answer the following questions:
1 Where and what height is the highest point on the map?
2 What height is Plaiskin Farm (966454)?
3 What height is the road junction at 964427?
4 Is most of Derrykeighan (9633) above or below 50m?

Mapwork

All these photographs were taken in the map area. Try to give a six figure grid reference for each one.

1. Dunseverick Castle
2. Giant's Causeway Visitor Centre
3. Bushmills B66 / Ballycastle (B67) Moss-Side Dervock B66
4. Parish of Billy · Diocese of Connor
5. "Old Bushmills" Distillery Co Ltd
6. Straidbilly Primary School

11

Mapwork

All these photographs were also taken in the map area.
Try to give a six figure grid reference for each one.

The answers are on the Colourpoint web site at www.colourpoint.co.uk/Educational/homeground.html

Ecosystems

An **ecosystem** includes weather, climate, soil, animals and plants in an area. These all work together in a community to form the ecosystem. **Soil** is an important part of any ecosystem. Without it we would not be able to grow any food. Without food people cannot live in an area. The soil in an area depends partly on its **weather** and **climate** (see page 32). It also depends on the rocks of the area and the way they are eroded and weathered (see pages 20 - 22). The **animals** and **plants** that grow up depend on the climate, weather and soil which they find there. The sun powers all ecosystems. Without it there would be no life on Earth.

Ecosystems

In Northern Ireland we have different kinds of ecosystems in different areas. The cliffs of Fair Head in County Antrim have different plants and animals to those in a hedgerow in County Tyrone. The animals and plants found in a peat bog in the Antrim mountains would not survive a move to a forest like Tollymore or Gortin Glen. The insects and fish that live in Lough Neagh would die if you were to take them to Strangford Lough. Can you think why this would happen?

Resource A ▶

Exercises

Match the photographs, in Resource A, of six common ecosystems in Northern Ireland to the descriptions below.

| Mountain | Cliff | Sand dune | Hedgerow | Lake | Forest |

Ecosystems

Food Chains

Food chains are found in all ecosystems. A food chain is formed as animals eat plants and other animals. There is always an animal, bird, or person at the top of a food chain. Resource B shows two simple food chains common in Northern Ireland.

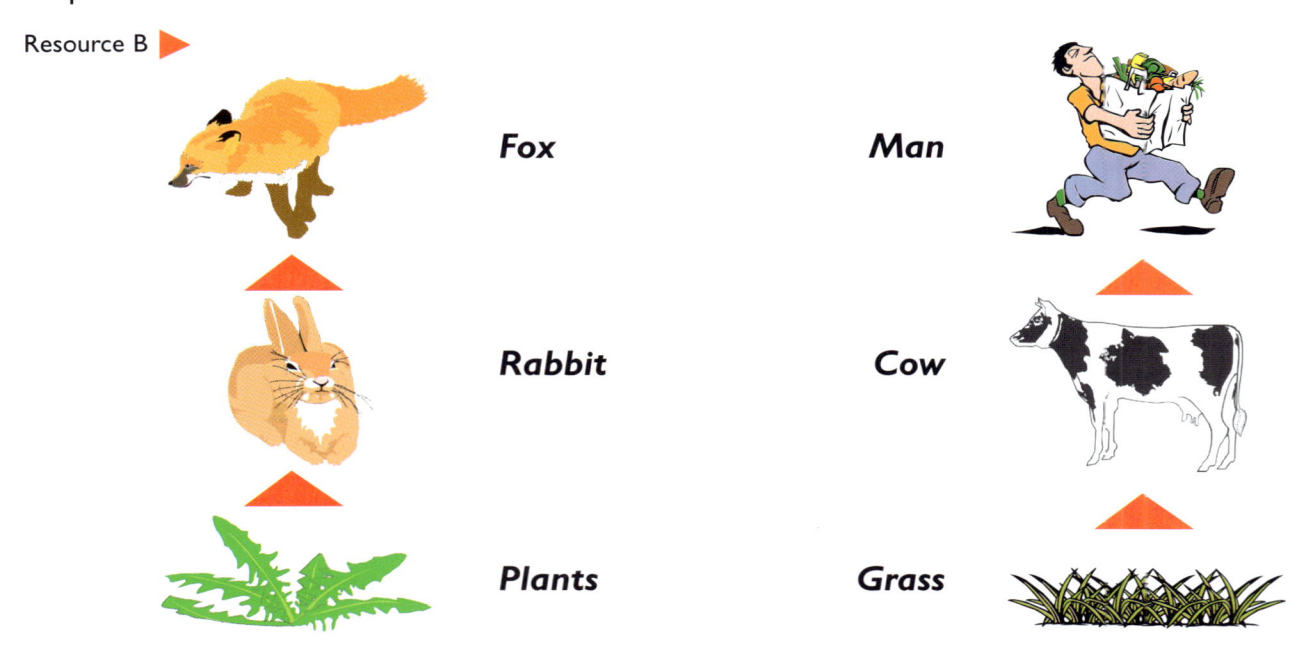

Resource B ▶

Fox
▲
Rabbit
▲
Plants

Man
▲
Cow
▲
Grass

What will happen if farmers trap and kill all the foxes in an area?

Resource C shows two food chains found in ecosystems within Northern Ireland. The first food chain is found in freshwater lakes like Lough Neagh or Lough Erne. The second food chain is found in forests like Tollymore, County Down, or Ballypatrick, County Antrim. These are simple food chains; in real life they will be much more complicated and will often overlap.

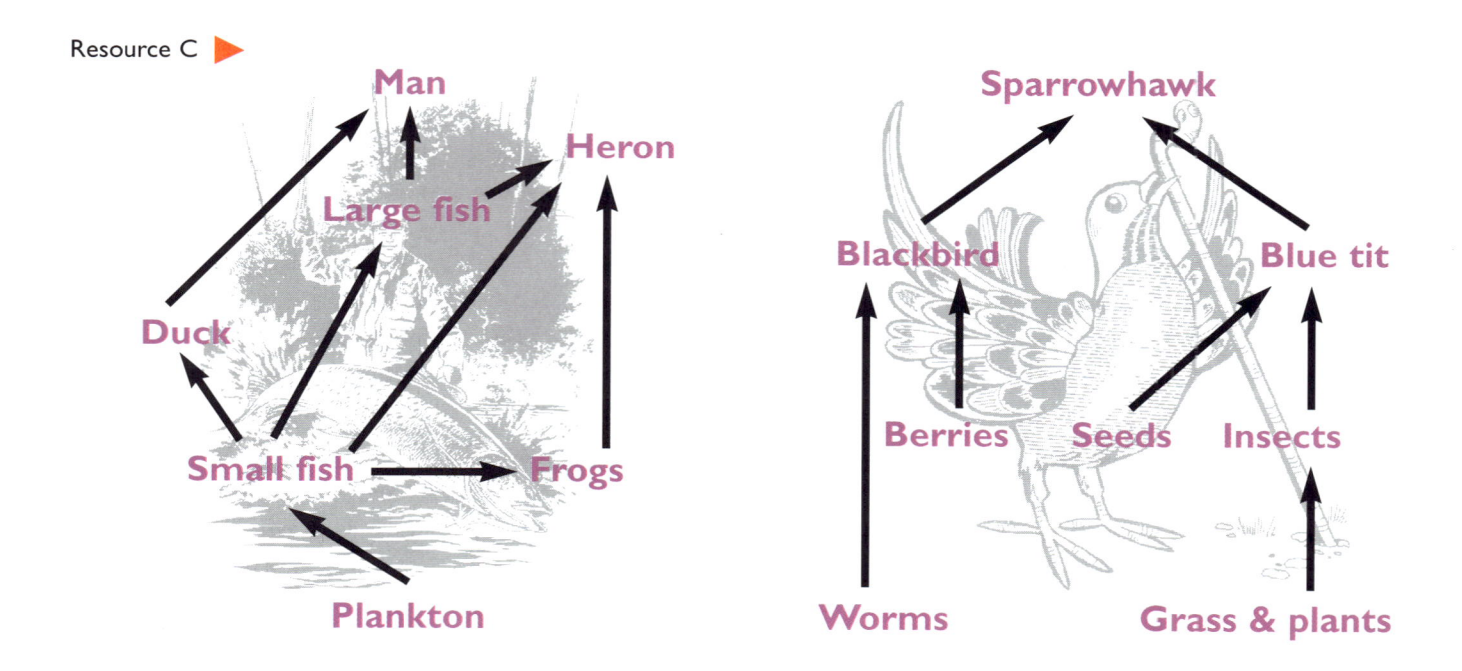

Resource C ▶

Man, Heron, Large fish, Duck, Small fish, Frogs, Plankton

Sparrowhawk, Blackbird, Blue tit, Berries, Seeds, Insects, Worms, Grass & plants

Ecosystems

Look at Resource D; this shows some of the links in an ecosystem. You can see that it is a very complicated system and almost everything is connected. If something happens to one part, then other parts will be affected.

Resource D ▼

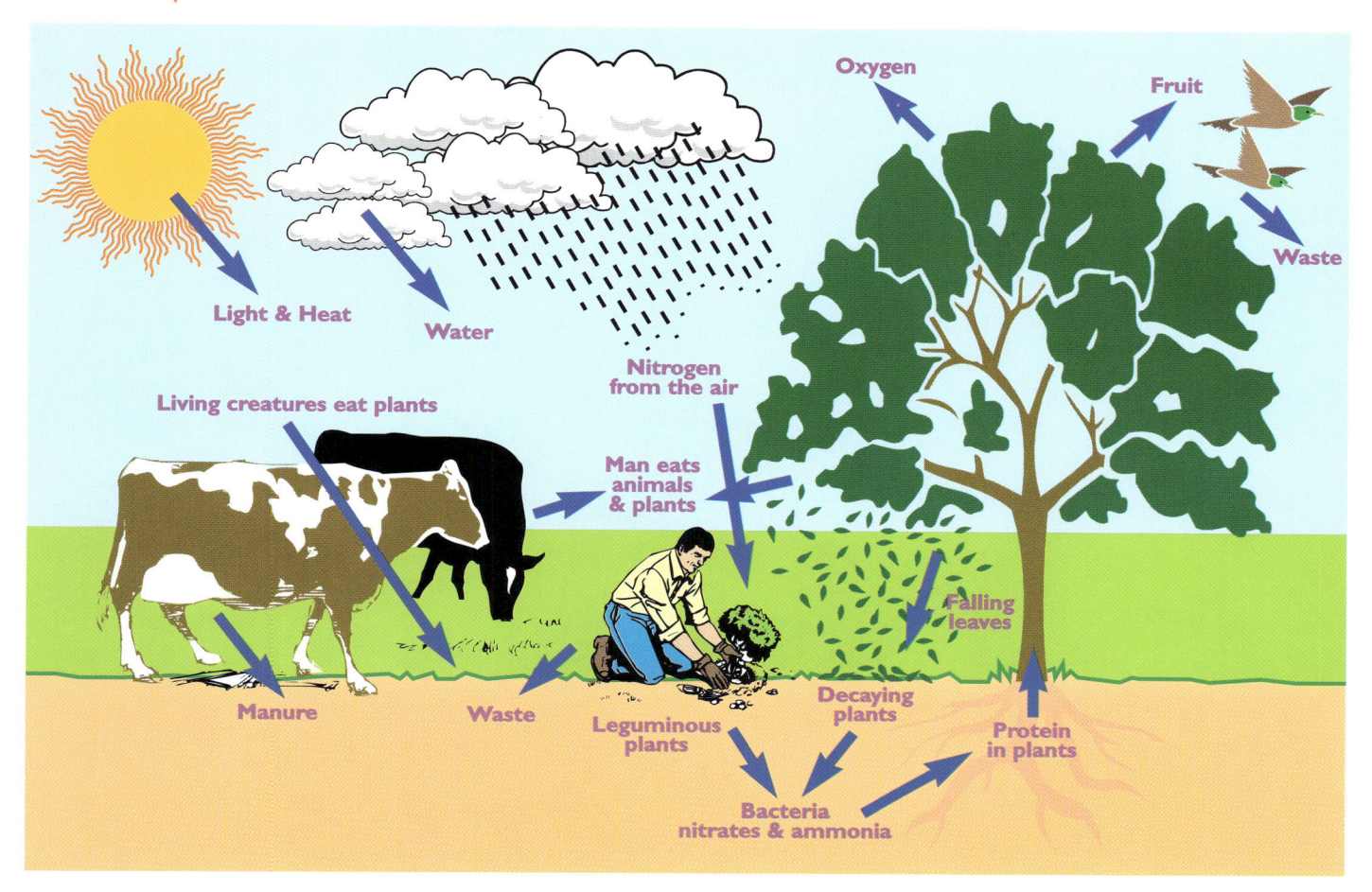

Exercises

Look at the ecosystem shown in Resource D and answer the following questions:

1. What would happen if there was a drought, ie no rain for a long time?
2. If man sprayed the grass with weedkiller, what would happen to the insects and animals?
3. If the trees were cut down, what would happen to the bird life?
4. If a volcanic eruption blocked out light from the sun, how might this effect the system?
5. Look at the photograph of the hedgerow on page 13.
   (a) Give two reasons why the farmer might decide to remove this hedgerow.
   (b) Say how this would affect the insects and animals that live there.
   (c) The farmer replaces the hedgerow with a barbed wire fence. Suggest two reasons why he might do this.

Humans can have a big effect on ecosystems. As well as removing hedges, humans can cut down trees, drain marshes, dig up peat for fuel, deepen rivers, drain ponds, and build houses and roads. Each action has an effect on the insects, plants and animals that live there. The area where they live is called their **habitat**. Sometimes it is possible for the wildlife to move somewhere else but sometimes they have nowhere else to go and they will be unable to breed. If their habitat is destroyed, then the animal, plant or insect species will die out.

Ecosystems

Soil

Physical environments (page 18) and weather (page 30) combine to give the soil you find in an area. Soil does not form overnight; it may take hundreds of years for a soil to form. Soil is formed when rock breaks down and weathers into tiny pieces. This is then mixed up with other ingredients to give a soil. Resource E shows the different ingredients that make up a soil.

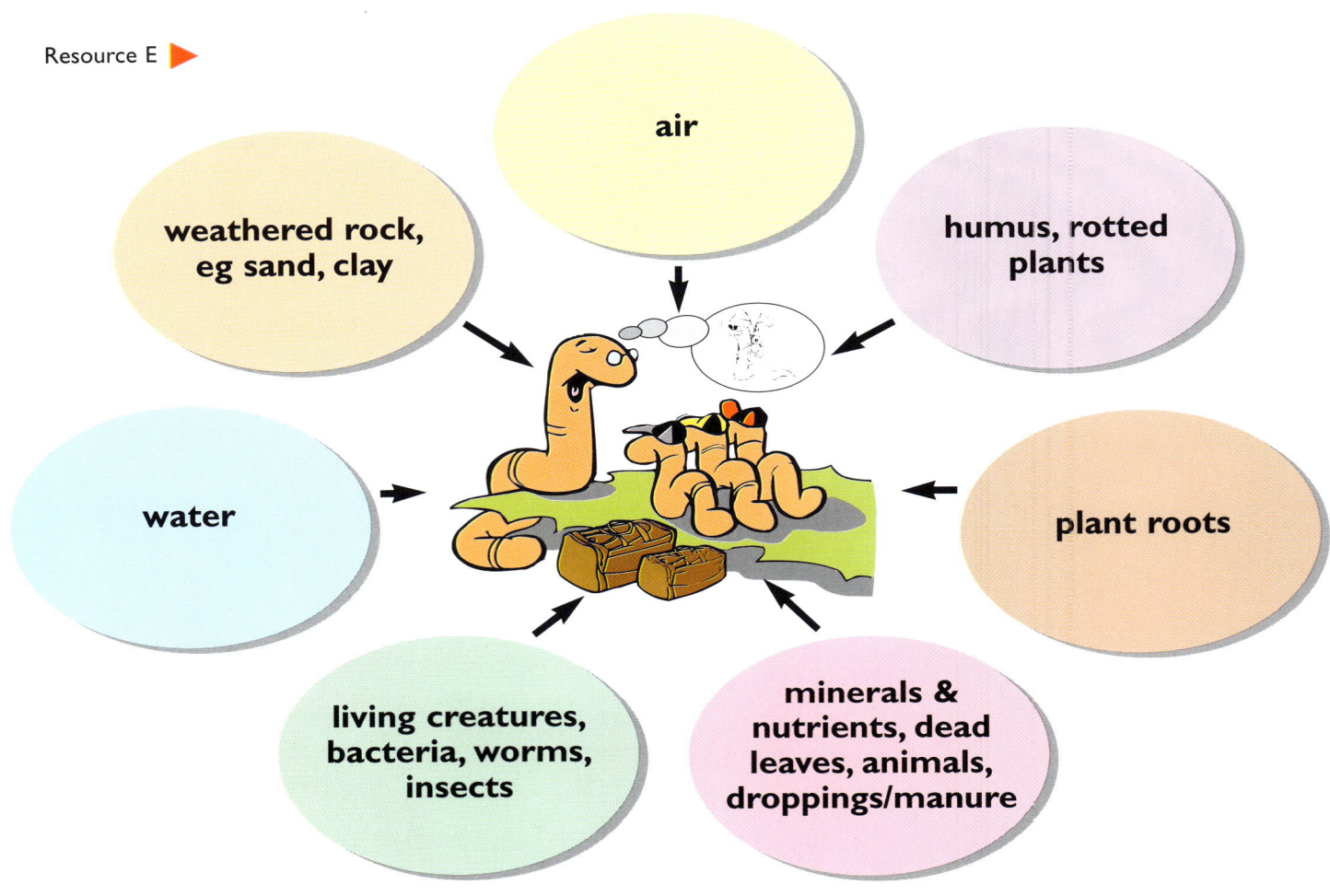

Resource E ▶

- air
- weathered rock, eg sand, clay
- humus, rotted plants
- water
- plant roots
- living creatures, bacteria, worms, insects
- minerals & nutrients, dead leaves, animals, droppings/manure

If these ingredients are present in different amounts then you will get a different type of soil. A fertile soil will have a lot of humus, while a poor soil will have less humus. Clay soils can hold a lot of water while sandy soils allow water to escape. The plants that grow in each soil will also be different. Some plants only grow in a certain type of soil and if that soil is very rare, then the plants which grow in it will also be rare.

Exercises

Farmers can alter soil to improve it. Copy the following table into your book and opposite each heading say what the farmer could do to improve his soil.

Problem	What the farmer can do
Soil is too dry	??
Soil is too wet	??
Soil does not have enough air	??
Soil does not have enough humus	??
Soil does not have enough minerals and nutrients	??

Ecosystems

Soils are not always the same depth. Some soils are over two metres deep, while other places have no soil at all, or a very thin soil which does not support a lot of plants. If we cut down through the soil, we can see what it is like and how deep it is. This is called a **soil profile**. A soil profile normally has three layers or **horizons**. These are shown on Resource F.

Resource F ▼

Vegetation cover of deciduous trees and grass

Amount of humus increases
Stone size increases

Grass and dead leaves

A **Topsoil**, *plant roots and much soil life*

B **Subsoil**, *fewer plant roots and less soil life*

C **Underlying rock** or *parent material*

The rock or parent material is one of the main ingredients of a soil. If the rock underneath is sandstone then the soil will be sandy. Chalk underneath will give a chalky soil. The best type of soil is a loam, where there is a good mixture of all the ingredients.

Exercises

Look at the Ordnance Survey Map on page 8. The map contains examples of several ecosystems mentioned in this chapter. Try to match the ecosystem in the left-hand column to the map reference in the right-hand column.

Ecosystem	Map reference
1 Cliff	Square 9643
2 Sand dunes	960360
3 River	937426
4 Wood	955454
5 Lake	940389
6 Farmland	955446

Physical geography

This section is concerned with the Earth we live on – the rocks below our feet and the shape of the land around us. We are thinking especially about Northern Ireland in this section, but we must always remember that Northern Ireland is only one small part of the Earth. Before we focus on Northern Ireland we need to find out a little bit more about the Earth. Look at Resource A which shows what the Earth is like when sliced through the centre like a piece of fruit.

Resource A ▶

The diagram shows that there are three main parts to the Earth:

The core
This is the centre of the Earth. It is extremely hot and is probably solid.

The mantle
This is a layer of molten (melted) rock called magma; it is 1000 °C.

The crust
This is the hard outer shell of the Earth and it is the part we live on. If the Earth were like a peach, the skin of the peach would represent the thickness of the crust.

The crust is the part of the Earth that we live on; it is made up of many different types of rocks. Some of these rocks make up Northern Ireland, so they are important to us because they form the ground under our feet. Look at Resource B on page 19. It shows some of the rocks which are found in Northern Ireland. By looking at the rocks we can identify them and tell where they come from.

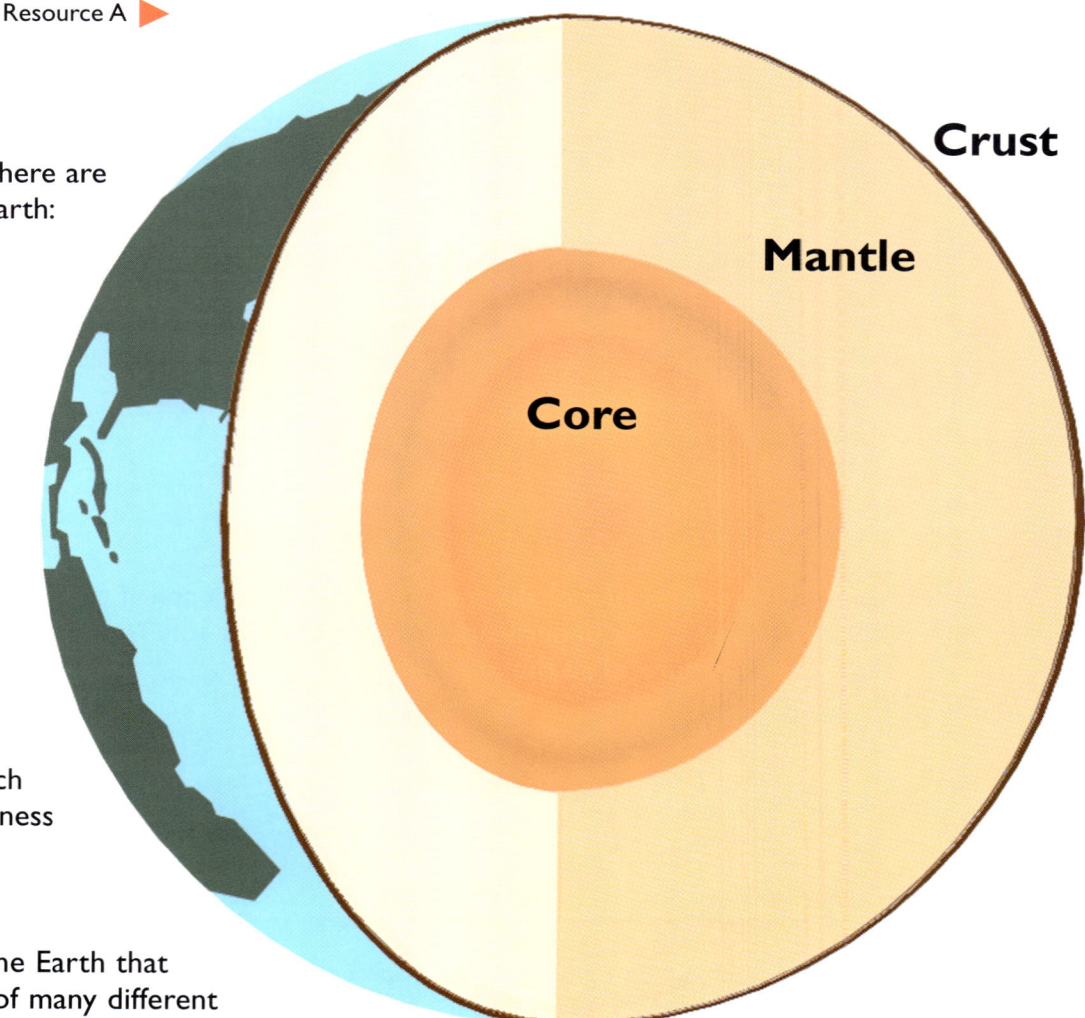

www.bbc.co.uk/education/rocks/index.shtml
www.bwctc.northants.sch.uk/website/html/projects/science/ks34/rocks/list.html

Physical geography

Identifying Rocks

Here are photographs of some of the more important rocks in Northern Ireland.

Beside each one is a description of the rock.

Resource B ▶

Chalk Chalk is a white rock and sometimes contains **fossils** – the remains of animals and plants preserved in the rock. The best place to see chalk is at White Park Bay or the White Rocks near Portrush. There is chalk all the way along the Antrim Coast Road north of Larne and there is a chalk quarry at Glenarm. It is used in the chemical industry, for making cement and for liming fields.

Basalt This is a black rock which sometimes has white crystals in it. The Giant's Causeway and most of the Antrim Plateau are made of basalt. It is quarried and used as road fill.

Sandstone This is a reddish brown rock. It is rough to touch and if you rub it, it will rub away in your hand. The best place to see it is Scrabo Quarry outside Newtownards. It was quarried for building and fireplaces. Scrabo Tower and Newtownards Town Hall are made from this rock.

Limestone There are many different types of limestone ranging from nearly white to cream, yellow and grey. It dissolves in water and can form underground cave systems like those found at Marble Arch Caves in County Fermanagh. It can be quarried and used in chemicals and cement. Limestone often contains fossils as it is made up from the bones of long dead animals.

Granite There are lots of different types of granite. This is Mourne granite and it is found in the Mourne Mountains. It is a speckled rock with different minerals in it. You can see black, white, grey and silver in Mourne granite. It is used in building, kerbstones and gravestones. The huge boulders which protect the Tropicana Centre in Newcastle from the sea are made of Mourne granite.

19

Physical geography

Resources

Rocks provide us with many of the things we need and use from day to day – these are called **resources** – something obtained from the Earth, which can be used by man. Resources can be divided in two.
Renewable resources can be used over and over again, eg trees or fish.
Non-renewable resources cannot be replaced once they run out, eg coal or oil.

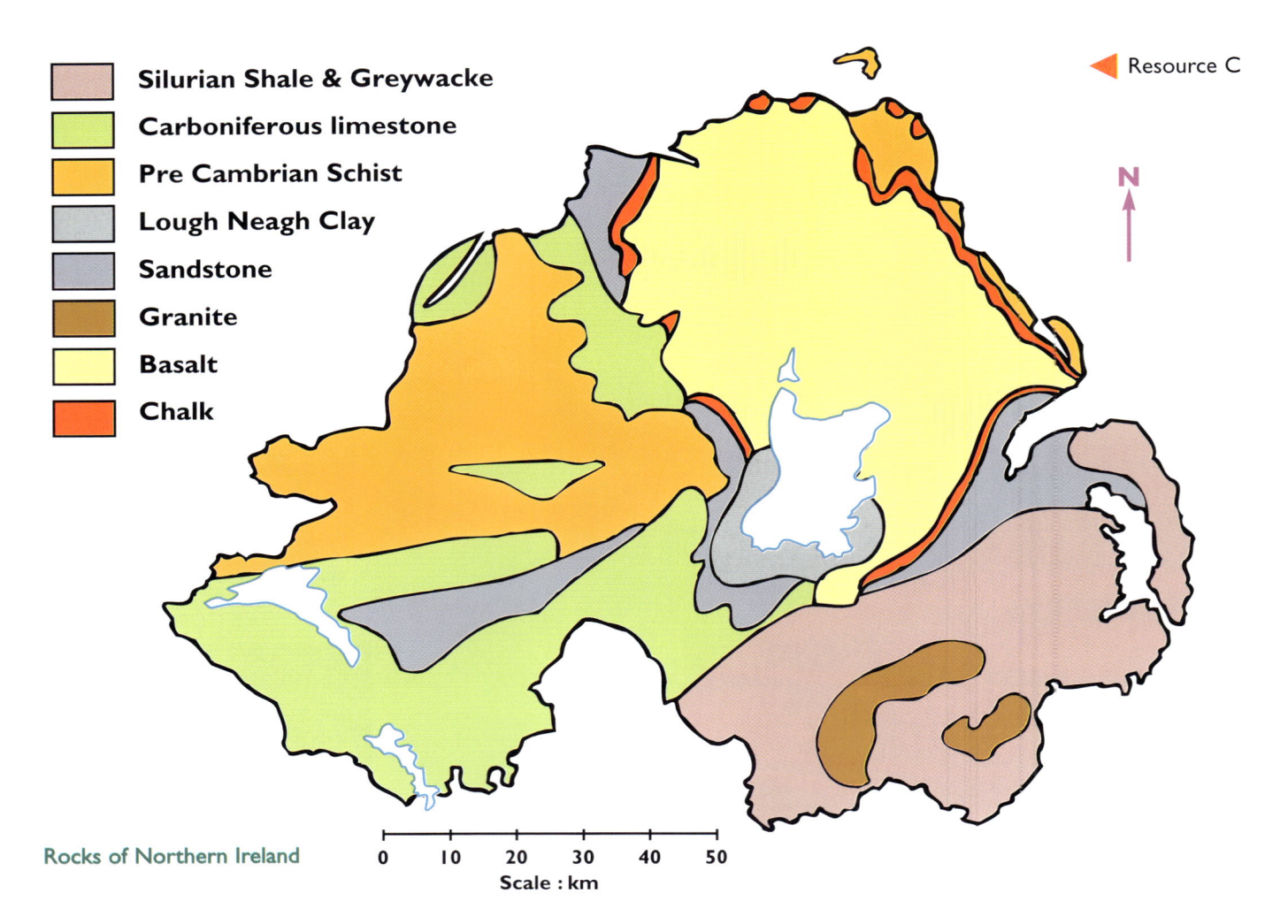

Legend:
- Silurian Shale & Greywacke
- Carboniferous limestone
- Pre Cambrian Schist
- Lough Neagh Clay
- Sandstone
- Granite
- Basalt
- Chalk

Resource C

Rocks of Northern Ireland
Scale : km (0 10 20 30 40 50)

Northern Ireland is not well off for resources. Many of the valuable resources found in rocks are not found in Northern Ireland and have to be imported, eg coal, oil and iron ore.

Exercises

1. Draw two columns in your book titled **Renewable** and **Non-renewable**. Look at the list of resources below and try to put them in the correct column.

    | IRON ORE | SOIL | WATER | GOLD | WHEAT |
    | TREES | FISH | SILVER | COFFEE | ALUMINIUM |
    | AIR | OIL | SANDSTONE | COAL | POTATOES |

2. Rewrite the following paragraph about rocks in Northern Ireland, choosing the best option from the two words given in italics.

    Northern Ireland is made up of many different types of rocks. In the north-east is a large area of *granite/basalt*. County Fermanagh contains a lot of *limestone/sandstone*. The Mourne Mountains are made of *granite/basalt*, while most of *County Down/Londonderry* is shale and greywacke. Rocks are a *renewable/non-renewable* resource and the rocks found in Northern Ireland are *valuable/not valuable*. *Granite/chalk* is the best rock for finding fossils, and this is common in County Antrim.

Physical geography

Three types of rock

All rocks can be divided into three types depending on how they are formed.

IGNEOUS

The first type of rock is called igneous rock. These are "fire-made" rocks formed from magma which has reached the surface of the Earth. The Earth's crust is not all one piece; it is divided into sections or plates like a giant jigsaw. Sometimes magma comes up to the surface between the plates and flows over the surface from a volcano or lava flow. When the magma cools it forms new rock. The main igneous rocks found in Northern Ireland are **basalt, granite** and **dolerite**.

SEDIMENTARY

The second type of rock is called sedimentary rock. These are "layered" rocks formed from other rocks which have been eroded and weathered by rain, rivers and seas, and then transported and deposited under the sea (see pages 22 and 23). Over time they sink into the crust and form new rock. The main sedimentary rocks found in Northern Ireland are **chalk, limestone, clay, shale, greywacke** and **sandstone**.

METAMORPHIC

The third type of rock is called metamorphic rock. These are "changed" rocks, which started off as igneous or sedimentary rocks but have been changed by being partly melted again. This happens either because they are close to a volcano or because they sink through the crust close to the mantle. The main metamorphic rocks in Northern Ireland are **schist** and **gneiss** (pronounced *nice*).

www.volcanoes.com
http://wwwneic.cr.usgs.gov/
http://www.gsrg.nmh.ac.uk/gsrg.html
http://volcano.und.nodak.edu

Exercises

Copy and complete the following paragraph using words from the wordbox below:

Rocks are divided into three types: _____, sedimentary and metamorphic. Northern Ireland contains examples of all three. The Mourne Mountains are made of _____, an igneous rock. The Giant's Causeway is made of _____ – another igneous rock. Scrabo Tower is built on a _____ hill although it has a dolerite cap. Sandstone is a _____ rock like limestone and _____. Metamorphic rocks are mainly found in Tyrone and _____. They are old hard rocks that are much used for quarrying.

| basalt | igneous | sedimentary | Londonderry | chalk | granite | sandstone |

Physical geography

Weathering and Erosion

Once rocks are laid down on the Earth's surface, they start to be worn away. This happens very slowly and gradually over a long period of time. We can see this around us where a dripping tap gradually wears a hole in the concrete, or a road has to be re-laid because it is slowly worn down by the traffic driving over it day by day. The wearing away of the Earth's surface in this way is called weathering and erosion.

Weathering happens when the weather attacks and wears away the rocks.

Erosion is the wearing away of the Earth's surface by the agents of erosion.

There are four types of weathering

Freeze thaw weathering
Onion skin weathering
Biological weathering *
Chemical weathering *

There are four agents of erosion

Rivers *
Ice
Sea *
Wind

*Only the ones with an asterisk are commonly found in Northern Ireland.
Your teacher will explain the other ones to you and we will look at some of the effects of those we find here.

Weathering

Biological weathering

This is the action of plants and animals in breaking down rocks. Plants grow and force their roots down into rock breaking it apart. Animals dig and burrow down into the ground gradually causing the rock to break apart. This happens in all areas and is happening now in your garden or in your school grounds.

Chemical weathering

This is when rainwater, which is a very weak acid, dissolves the rock in the same way that salt or sugar dissolve in water. Gradually a hole is worn in the rock. This happens especially in limestone and a whole cave system can be formed if the rock is worn away. The best example of this is the Marble Arch Caves in County Fermanagh.

Physical geography

Erosion

Agents of erosion wear away the rock, transport the debris and deposit it somewhere else.
In Northern Ireland, the two main agents of erosion are **rivers** and **sea**, although ice was important over 10,000 years ago.

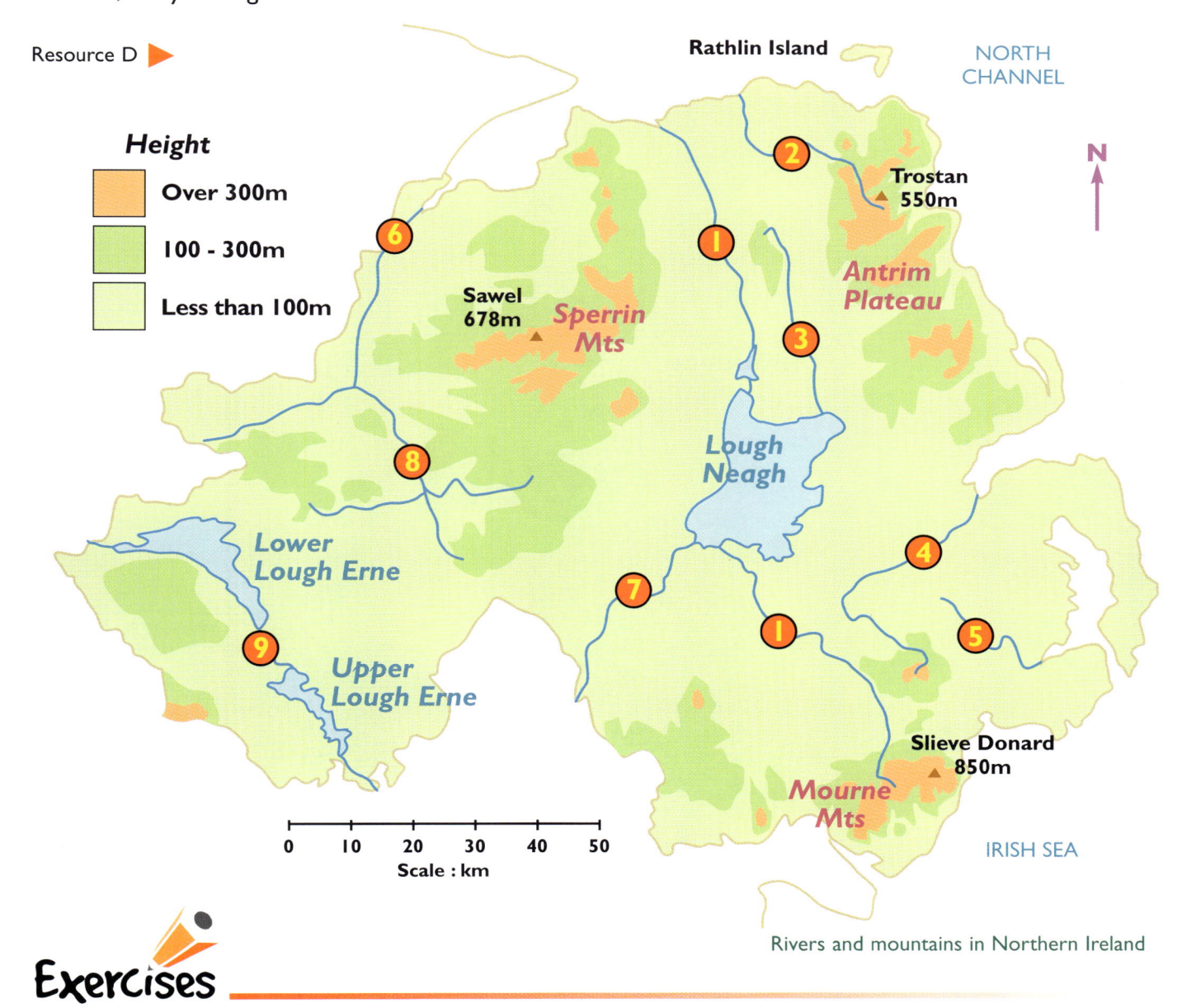

Resource D ▶

Rivers and mountains in Northern Ireland

Exercises

Rivers are very important in Northern Ireland. The names of some of the main rivers in Northern Ireland are in the table below but the letters are mixed up.

nabn	galan	loique
rackblewat	feloy	mani
rulest	shub	reen

Each river is marked on the map above (Resource D) with a number. Try to match the river to the correct number. Once you have sorted out the names of the rivers, try to say which county each is in and give the name of a settlement on each river. Use the map on page 4 and/or your atlas to help you.

23

Physical geography

Look at Resource E below which shows a river basin.

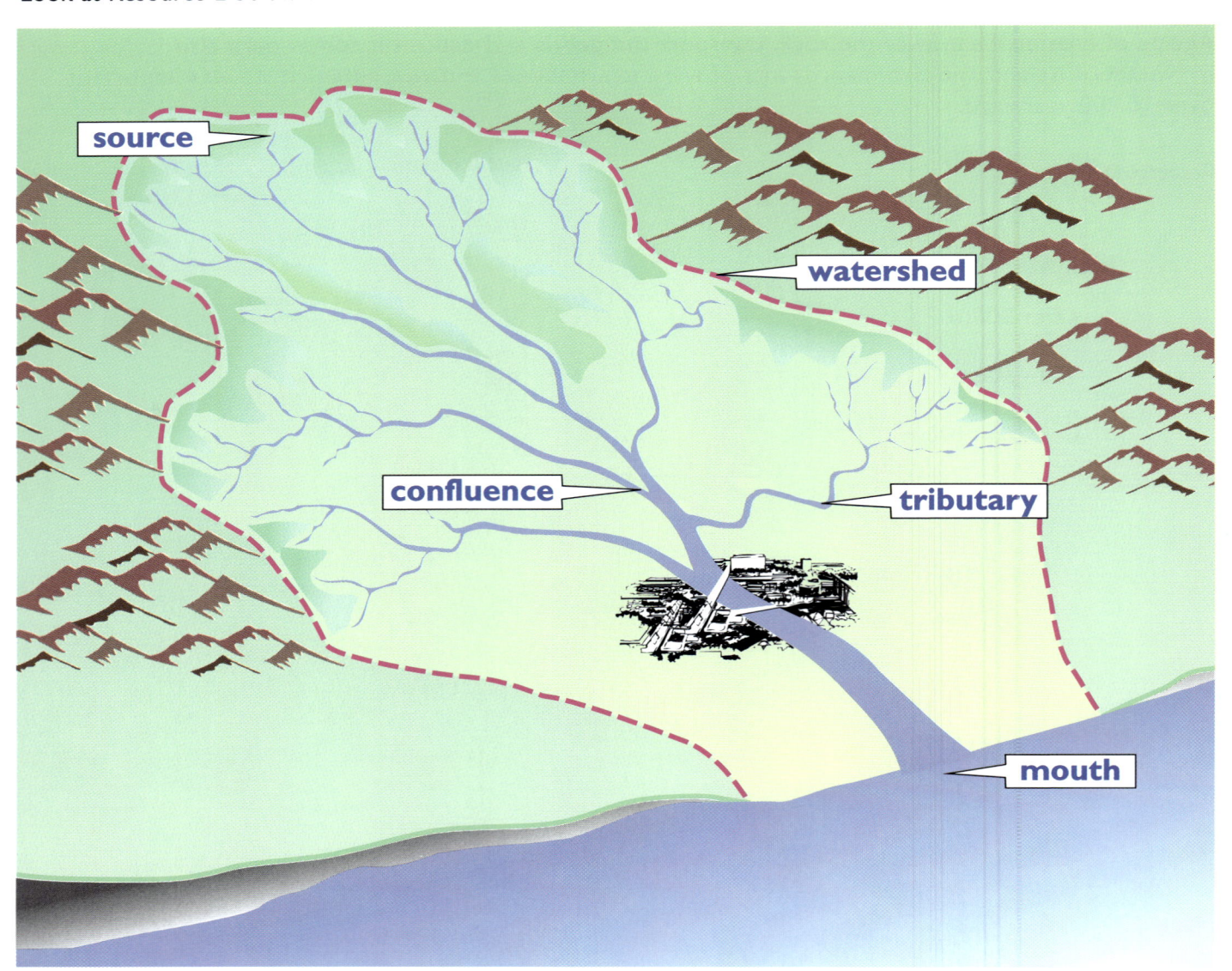

Resource E

http://community.labs.bt.com/public/WickhamMarketPublic/River_Home_Page.html
http://www.oneworld.org/ni/issue273/facts.html

Exercises

Match up the two lists, which give a river feature and its meaning:

The source	is where two rivers meet.
The mouth	is the area of highland, which forms the edge of a river basin.
The watershed	is a small river flowing into a larger river.
The river basin	is where the river starts.
A tributary	is where the river reaches a lake or the sea.
A confluence	is the area of land drained by a river and its tributaries.

Physical geography

River study

There is part of a river on the map extract on Page 8. This shows the lower course of the River Bush and the mouth of the river where it reaches the sea. Resource F shows the source of the Bush in the Antrim Hills over 48 km (30 miles) away. It is at a height of 480m. The surrounding land is heather moorland and is grazed only by sheep or used for forestry. All rivers, including the Bush, erode material from the bed and banks, transport it downstream and then deposit it on the bed of a sea or a lake.

Resource F ▶

[Photograph showing river near source with label "river erodes"]

Rivers erode vertically and horizontally, that is they cut down and out (see Resource F). Over time they wear away the valley which becomes deeper and wider. Compare Resource F, which is taken near the source, with Resource G which is taken further downstream. You can see that the river is wider and deeper and the banks are much lower. At this point the river is only 130m above sea level so the surrounding land is farmland. It is much better quality than the source and can be used for livestock or ploughed for crops.

Resource G ▶

[Photograph showing river further downstream with labels "erosion under bank", "channel", and "stones deposited"]

25

Physical geography

Resource H is taken at Seneirl Bridge at 943361 on the map extract on page 8. At this point the river is flowing through rich farmland and is wider and deeper. It is at a height of less than 30m and is only 8 km from the sea. In its lower course the river has less energy and is not eroding as much as it did nearer the source. It will still transport much material and will even begin to deposit some of its load if there is a drought. **Meanders** are another feature of the lower course of a river, where the river swings from side to side in a series of loops. These can be seen on the map extract in squares 9341 and 9339. Resource I shows what happens in a meander – the river erodes one side of the bend and deposits on the other side of the bend.

Resource H ▼

Resource I ▼

- river cliff
- slip off slope
- erosion deposition
- rivers swings to outside of bend

Resource J is taken at the mouth of the river (933424) where the Bush reaches the sea. Unlike many rivers, the Bush is fairly natural and has not been really changed by man. Most rivers have a large built up area round the mouth, eg Belfast, Derry, Coleraine, and have been lined with concrete and steel to ensure that they do not flood. The Bush enters the sea through a Golf Course so it has not been changed very much. At this point the river is dropping a lot of the material which it has transported from further upstream, and there is very little evidence of erosion.

Resource J ▶

Exercises

Look at Resource J and list the ways that man has changed the mouth of the River Bush.

Choose one of the five photographs of the River Bush and draw a sketch of the river. On your sketch, label the main features of the river. If you are unused to sketching, trace the main features instead and then label them.

Coastal Study

Resource K ▶

The sea also erodes, transports and deposits. Erosion of the coastline happens in various places, usually along cliffs and at headlands, but it can also occur on flat low-lying coastlines. Look at Resource K which shows the coastline of County Down at Ballyhalbert. In the early 1900s the cottages used to have gardens on the other side of the road where the beach is now. The sea has eroded the gardens, and to prevent further erosion, people have put up defences to prevent the sea eroding the road, or even worse, the houses. The material eroded by the sea is swept further along the coast and deposited on Ballyhalbert beach – see Resource L. Deposition of material means that the harbour can only be used at high tide.

Resource L ▶

Physical geography

Resource M ▶

Erosion is also happening along the north coast of County Antrim between Fair Head and Magilligan Point. This usually happens in stages as the sea attacks the basalt and chalk cliffs. The waves batter into the cliffs, particularly in winter. They gradually erode the base of the cliff and open up a cave – see Resource M. The cave will become bigger and eventually the cliff above it will collapse into the sea. This happened at Dunluce Castle in 1639 (see Resource N), when the kitchens tumbled into the sea in a storm. The collapsed rock will protect the base of the cliff until the sea wears it away, when it can renew its attack on the cliff again.

Resource N ▶

Physical geography

Resource O ▼

Resource P ▼

Headlands, which sit out into the sea, can have a cave pushed through to form an arch. If the roof of the arch collapses a stack is left. The ever-active sea will eventually wear this away. Resource O shows an arch in chalk at the White Rocks near Portrush. Resource P shows a stack at the Giant's Causeway. (950452 on the OS Map on page 8). Material that has been eroded from these cliffs will be deposited on the many beaches along the coast. Photograph Q shows the beach at Portballintrae (9242 on the OS Map on page 8). The sand on the beach is made up of millions of tiny pieces of rock worn away from the surrounding cliffs and headlands. The beach can also be seen on page 12, photograph 8.

Resource Q ▶

29

Weather

Weather is something that affects everybody. Some people have jobs that are easier or harder depending on the weather. Pupils going to and from school are affected by the weather. Sports, games and transport are affected by the weather. Walking the dog, doing a paper round, drying washing or shopping are all easier if the weather is dry and warm. Cold and wet weather makes all these things harder. In some cases extreme weather can result in loss of life and millions of pounds of damage which has to be put right. Strong winds damage trees and houses, heavy rain causes floods and freezing temperatures cause accidents and put up fuel bills for everybody.

Recording the weather

Weather is made up of different things such as rain, wind and temperature. These are called the **elements of weather**, and they all have to be measured and recorded. There are five elements that most people will know about, but a **meteorologist** will look at other elements as well. Resource A shows the instruments used to measure these elements.

Resource A ▶

1 A **rain gauge** is used to measure the amount of rainfall. This is measured in mm every 24 hours.

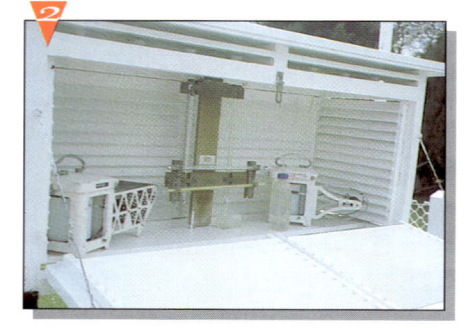

2 A **maximum-minimum thermometer** is used to measure temperature. The highest and lowest temperatures in the previous 24 hours are recorded in degrees Celsius (°C).

3 An **anemometer** is used to measure the speed of the wind. This is measured in km per hour.

5 The amount of cloud is measured using the naked eye. This is measured in eighths or oktas.

4 A **wind vane**, weather vane, or windsock is used to measure the direction of the wind. This is measured using the points of the compass.

The box in the middle of the diagram is called a **Stevenson Screen**. It holds the thermometers and keeps them out of the direct rays of the sun.

Weather

A meteorologist will want to know other things as well. When he puts all this information together then he will be able to predict the weather and issue a forecast for the daily newspapers, television and the Internet. Resource B shows some of the other elements and instruments.

Resource B ▼

cirrus

cumulus

stratus

The type of cloud is useful; this is measured by observation. There are ten different types of cloud, but they are based on three basic ones: cirrus, stratus and cumulus.

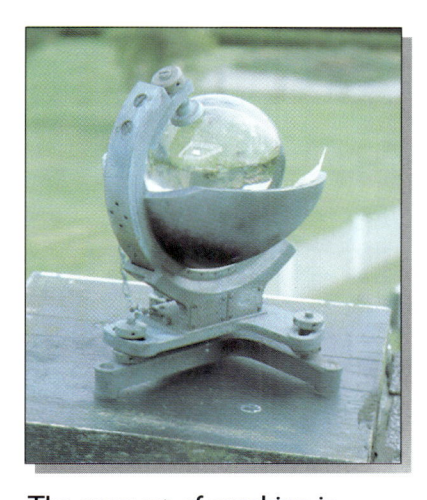

Frank Mitchell – weather man

The amount of sunshine is measured in hours using a **sunshine recorder**.

The air pressure, or weight, is measured using a **barometer**. It is measured in millibars. Falling pressure means that bad weather is on the way, rising pressure means that the weather is going to improve. Low pressure brings rain and wind; high pressure brings fine weather.

Visibility is measured in metres or kilometres. This is how far you can see. If mist or fog is present visibility is poor and can be less than 100m. In good visibility you can see 25 to 30 km.

Exercises

Copy and complete the table using some of the words from the word box below:

	Element of weather	Instrument used	Unit of measurement
1	Rainfall	??	mm
2	??	thermometer	in °C
3	Cloud amount	observation	??
4	Wind direction	??	compass points
5	Wind speed	anemometer	??
6	??	barometer	millibars
7	Sunshine	sunshine recorder	hours

| Pressure | rain gauge | oktas | cloud | km per hour | Temperature | wind vane | cirrus |

Weather

Weather and climate

Weather is recorded in thousands of weather stations all over the world. There are many weather stations in Northern Ireland. All the results are sent to the Meteorological Office who then use the data to predict weather and issue forecasts. They also keep records of the data so that they can look back and see what patterns there have been in the past. They can tell if records have been broken. They can also tell if rainfall or temperatures have been below or above average. Looking at patterns over the year means looking at climate. It is important to know the difference between weather and climate.

Weather is what happens day to day in the air around us.

Climate is the pattern over the year, worked out from 30 year averages.

Northern Ireland's climate is **temperate**. This means that it is not too hot and not too cold. Here are the climate figures for Aldergrove. These are based on records taken over at least 30 years.

ALDERGROVE	J	F	M	A	M	J	J	A	S	O	N	D	
Temperature (°C)	4	4	6	8	11	13	15	14	12	9	6	5	Range 11
Rainfall (mm)	83	55	59	51	56	65	79	78	82	85	75	84	Total 852 mm

Source: www.worldclimate.com

Exercises

Other parts of the world have different climates. Here are climate figures for three other places in the world: a desert, a tropical rain forest and an Arctic island. Say which place belongs to which diagram.

STATION X	J	F	M	A	M	J	J	A	S	O	N	D	
Temperature (°C)	26	26	26	26	26	26	27	27	28	28	27	27	Range 2
Rainfall (mm)	264	262	298	283	204	103	67	46	63	111	161	220	Total 2082 mm

STATION Y	J	F	M	A	M	J	J	A	S	O	N	D	
Temperature (°C)	-23	-26	-25	-18	-5	3	6	4	-2	-10	-16	-23	Range 32
Rainfall (mm)	7	8	4	4	5	6	14	17	13	11	11	5	Total 105 mm

STATION Z	J	F	M	A	M	J	J	A	S	O	N	D	
Temperature (°C)	14	17	21	25	31	36	37	37	33	27	20	14	Range 23
Rainfall (mm)	2	3	1	2	0	0	0	0	1	2	1	3	Total 15 mm

Source: www.worldclimate.com

Weather

LONGON *Heathrow Airport*	J	F	M	A	M	J	J	A	S	O	N	D	
Temperature (°C)	5	5	7	9	13	16	18	18	15	12	8	6	Range 13
Rainfall (mm)	62	36	50	43	45	46	46	44	43	73	45	60	Total 593 mm

Source: www.worldclimate.com

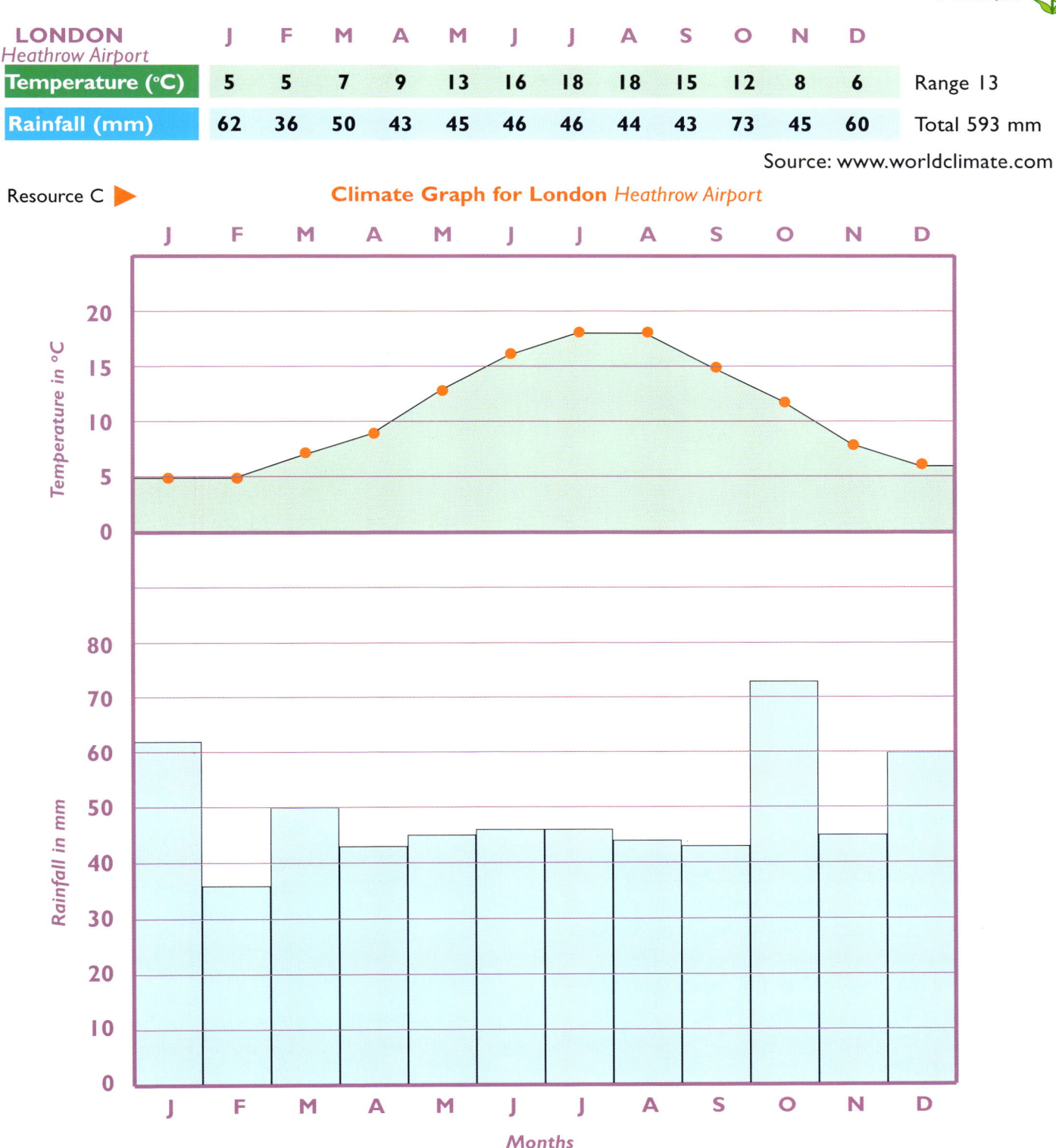

Resource C ▶ **Climate Graph for London** *Heathrow Airport*

Exercises

Look at Resource C. It is a climate graph for London. The rainfall is drawn using a bar graph at the bottom, the temperature is plotted above it using a line graph. Draw two more climate graphs in your book, one for Aldergrove and one for either Station X, Y or Z opposite. Compare the graphs for London and Aldergrove and you will see that they are slightly different. This tells us that even though places are close together on a world map they can have a slightly different climate and different weather. Even in Ireland there will be small differences between different places depending on where they are.

Weather

Resource D

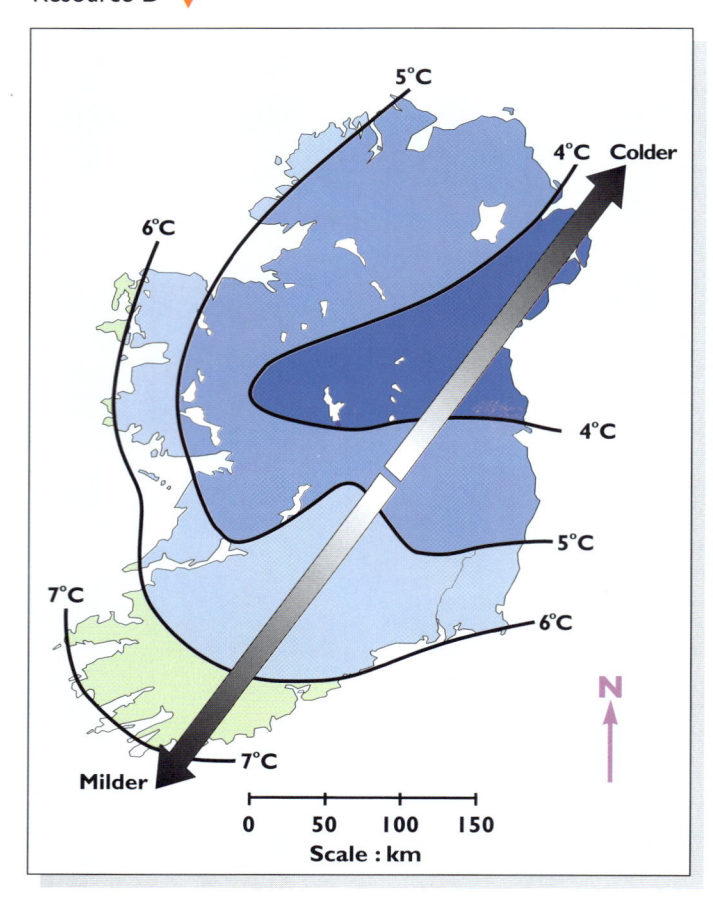

January average temperatures

Resource E

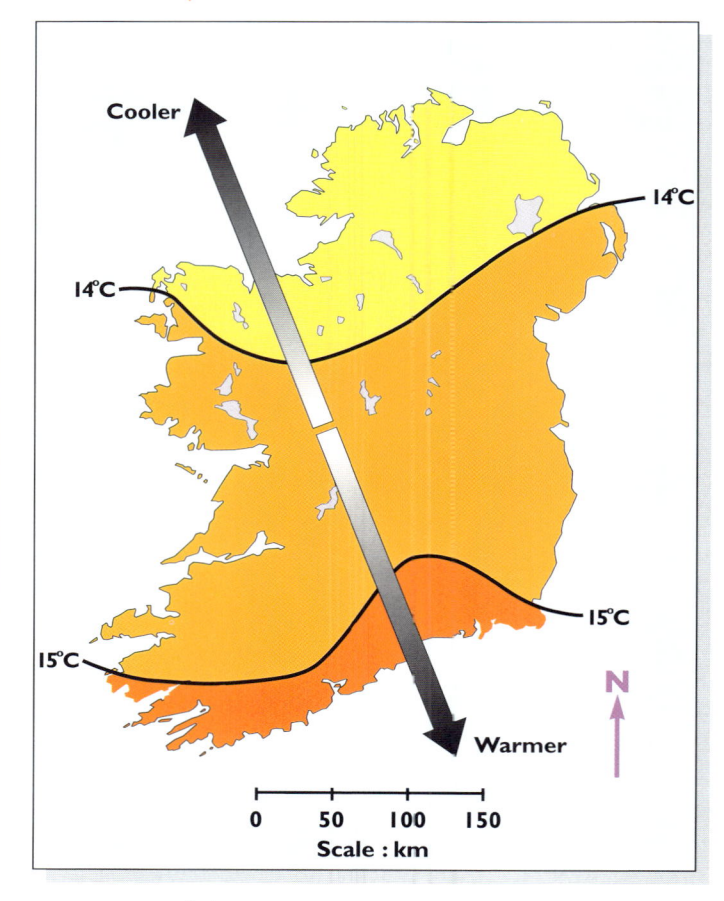

July average temperatures

Weather patterns in Ireland

Resource D shows the average temperatures in January. The warmest part of Ireland is the south-west. The coldest part is the north-east. Nowhere in Ireland is really cold even in January. The temperature falls below freezing point only for a day or two at a time, and the average temperatures do not show this. Winter in Ireland is cool rather than cold.

Resource E shows the average temperatures in July. The warmest part of Ireland is the south coast. The coolest part is the north. Nowhere in Ireland is really hot even in July. Any hot spells rarely last for more than one or two weeks and so don't influence the thirty year averages. Summer in Ireland is mild rather than warm.

Interesting Fact

The sun gives us light and heat (see page 13), but did you know that the Earth orbits the sun in one year at a speed of 29 km per second, or over 100,000 km per hour?

Interesting Fact

The Earth also revolves around its own axis once every 24 hours at a speed of over 1600 km per hour at the Equator.

Resource F

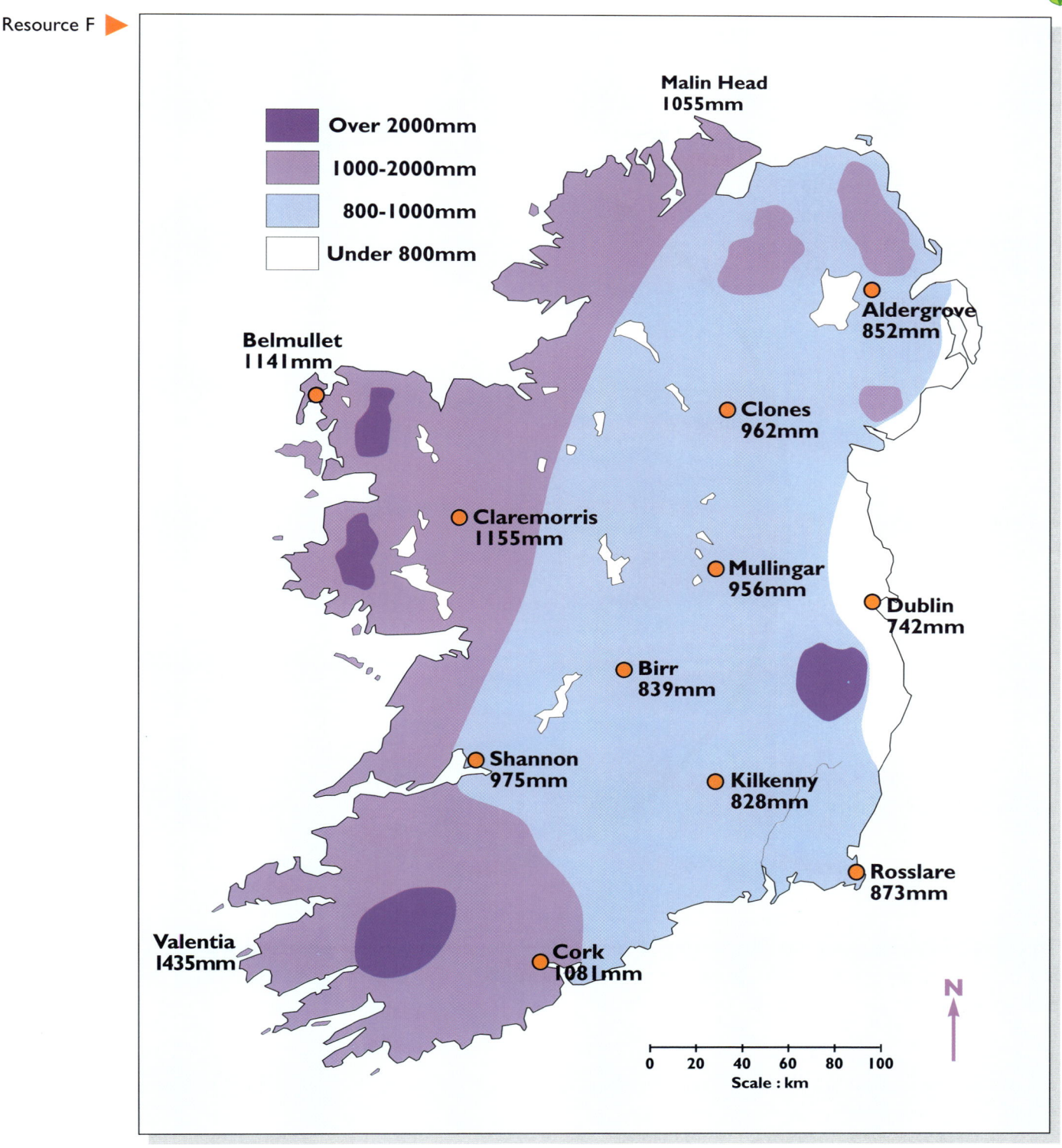

Weather

Legend:
- Over 2000mm
- 1000-2000mm
- 800-1000mm
- Under 800mm

Rainfall stations:
- Malin Head 1055mm
- Aldergrove 852mm
- Belmullet 1141mm
- Clones 962mm
- Claremorris 1155mm
- Mullingar 956mm
- Dublin 742mm
- Birr 839mm
- Shannon 975mm
- Kilkenny 828mm
- Rosslare 873mm
- Valentia 1435mm
- Cork 1081mm

Average annual rainfall (mm)

Resource F shows the average rainfall total over the year. The wettest areas are the highest mountains, especially in the west. The driest areas are in the east. Over most of Ireland rainfall is moderate, not too wet and not too dry, unless you live in one of the hilly areas. There is no seasonal pattern to the rain; it can come at any time of the year. If you look again at the climate figures for Aldergrove on page 32 you will see that July and August are wetter than some of the winter months.

Weather

What causes our climate and weather?

Our climate and weather are a result of four factors which all combine to give us the pattern we see on the three maps on page 34 and 35.

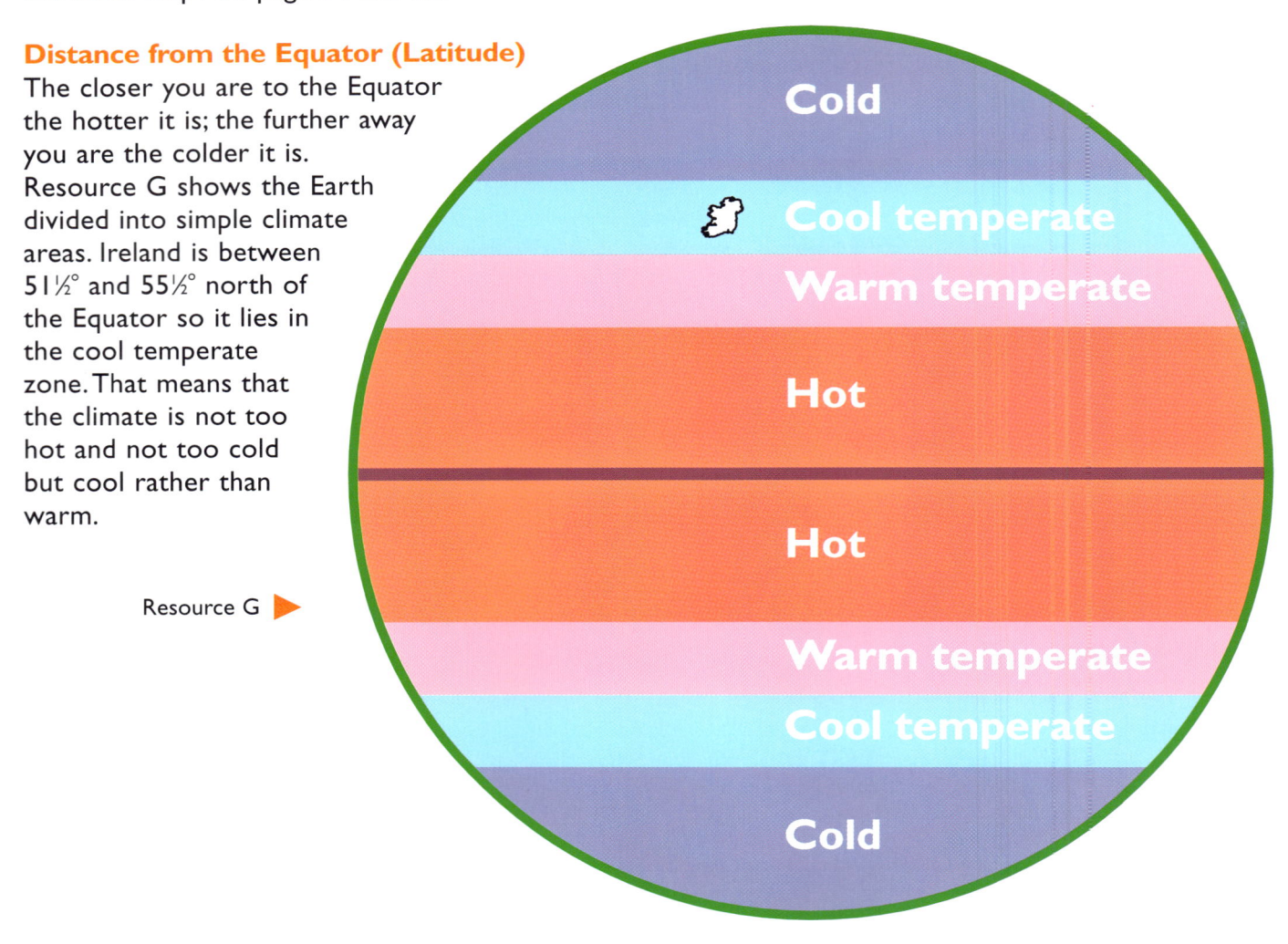

Distance from the Equator (Latitude)

The closer you are to the Equator the hotter it is; the further away you are the colder it is. Resource G shows the Earth divided into simple climate areas. Ireland is between 51½° and 55½° north of the Equator so it lies in the cool temperate zone. That means that the climate is not too hot and not too cold but cool rather than warm.

Resource G ▶

Cold
Cool temperate
Warm temperate
Hot
Hot
Warm temperate
Cool temperate
Cold

Altitude (Height above sea level)

The higher up you go the colder it gets. Every 150m you climb the temperature will drop by 1°C. Resource H shows what will happen to the temperature at the top of three mountains in Northern Ireland if the temperature is 15°C at sea level.

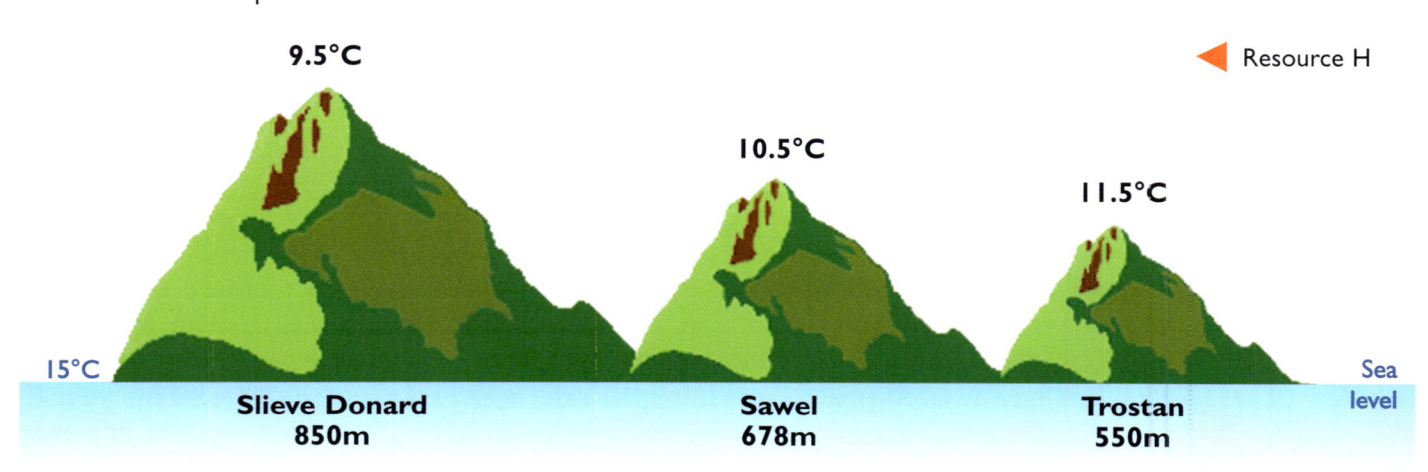

◀ Resource H

9.5°C — Slieve Donard 850m
10.5°C — Sawel 678m
11.5°C — Trostan 550m

15°C Sea level

Resource I

Air rises and cools

Cloud & rain

Warm moist air

Connemara Mts

Air descends & warms

Dublin

Atlantic Ocean

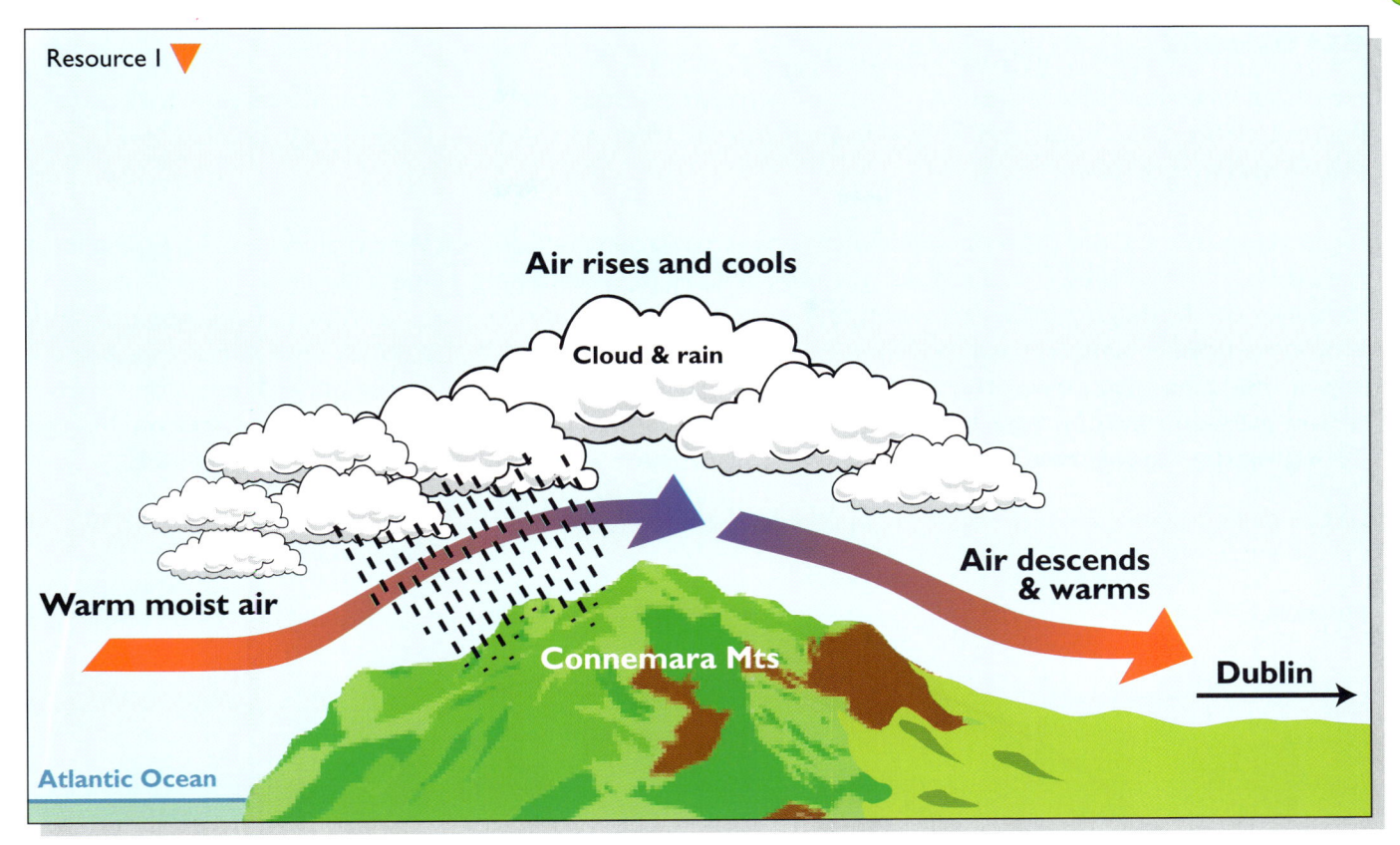

Prevailing wind (the direction the wind blows most of the time)
In Ireland the prevailing wind is from the west or south west 60% of the time (three days out of five). This wind blows from the Atlantic Ocean, which is a large mass of fairly warm water. The result of this is a wind that is mild in winter and warm in summer. It blows over a large area of sea so it picks up water and gives us quite a lot of rain (see Resource F on page 35).

Distance from the sea
Ireland is an island and is surrounded by the sea. This keeps us cooler in summer and warmer in winter than places which are far away from the sea. Look at the table below which shows climate figures for Valentia in Ireland, Berlin in Germany and Warsaw in Poland. Although they are roughly the same latitude, their climates are very different. Valentia is beside the sea, Berlin is further inland and Warsaw is still further away from the sea. An atlas map of Europe will let you see where Warsaw and Berlin are located.

Place	January average	July average	Range	Total rainfall
Valentia	7°C	15°C	8°C	1430mm
Berlin	-1°C	19°C	20°C	581mm
Warsaw	-4°C	19°C	23°C	550mm

The wind which brings Valentia so much rain blows east into Europe and by the time it reaches Berlin and Warsaw it does not have a lot of rain left. You can see that they are much drier. Resource I shows why we get a lot of rain compared to places further east.

Weather

Depressions

Most of our weather comes from **depressions** moving across the Atlantic Ocean. Weather forecasters talk about them quite often and they influence our weather all the time. They are also called low-pressure systems or lows.

Look at Resource J. Cold air from the Poles moves towards the Equator. Warm air from the Equator moves towards the Poles. The air does not mix; instead it meets along a line called the **Polar Front**. This marks the boundary between warm and cool areas. Unfortunately it is always shifting position and it is hard to predict where it will be even a day ahead. It moves north and south with the seasons and is rarely in the same place two days running. If the warm air pushes into the cold air, a depression forms. This low pressure system travels west to east along the Polar Front and quite often passes over Ireland. As a depression passes over, a sequence of weather occurs similar to that shown in Resource K.

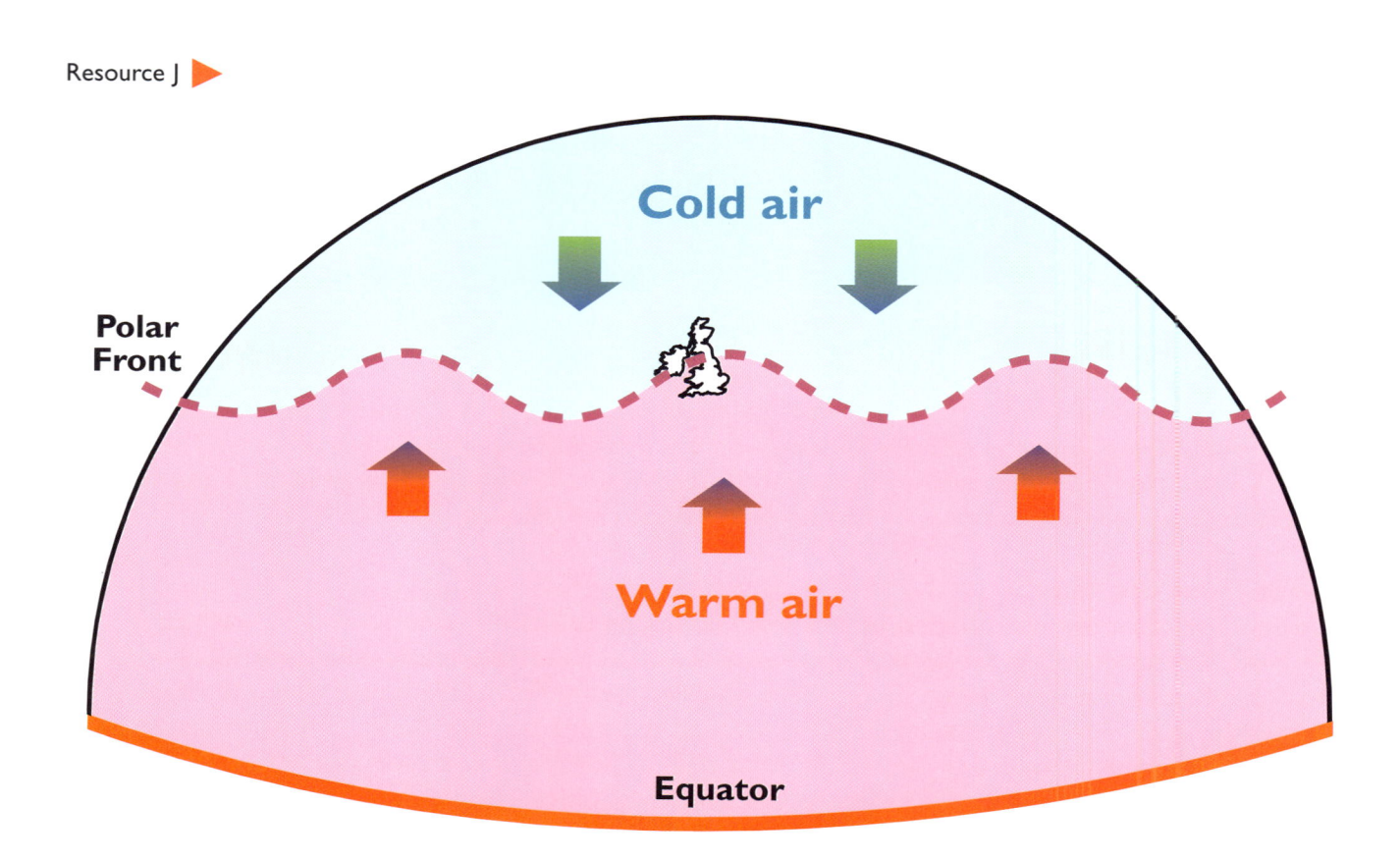

Resource J ▶

The Internet gives a lot of useful resources for the study of weather.
Satellite images can be found at:
www.nottingham.ac.uk/pub/sat-images/D2.JPG
www.met-office.gov.uk/satpics/latest_IR.html

Weather reports and information can be found at:
www.wunderground.com/global/uk.html
www.meto.gov.uk
http://weather.noaa.gov/weather/GB_cc.html
http://pcarx2.am.ub.es/infomet/arxiu/mapes_fronts/

Weather

Resource K

A depression

Low pressure

Rising air so clouds form

Unsettled weather

Strong winds

Winds blow anti-clockwise

Usually travels from west to east

Brings a sequence of weather

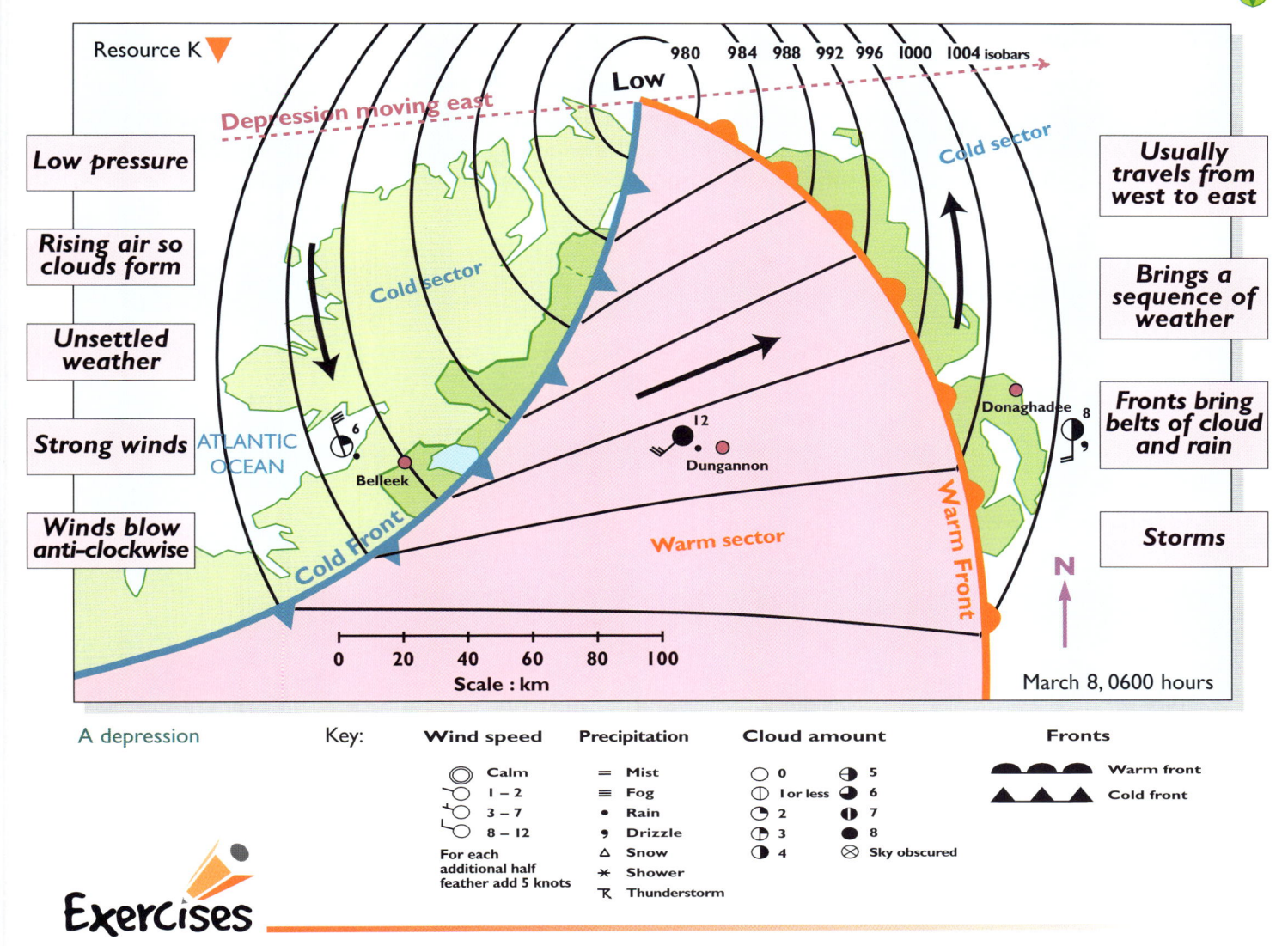

Fronts bring belts of cloud and rain

Storms

March 8, 0600 hours

Key:
- Wind speed: Calm, 1–2, 3–7, 8–12, For each additional half feather add 5 knots
- Precipitation: Mist, Fog, Rain, Drizzle, Snow, Shower, Thunderstorm
- Cloud amount: 0, 1 or less, 2, 3, 4, 5, 6, 7, 8, Sky obscured
- Fronts: Warm front, Cold front

Exercises

Copy and complete the following paragraph using words from the box below:

Depressions come from the ------------- Ocean. They travel over Ireland from -------- to --------. The wind blows in an ---------------- direction around the depression. They bring cloud, -------- and strong winds. The warm front arrives first bringing higher ------------ and lower pressure. The cloud cover increases and -------- falls. As the warm sector passes over the temperature remains high, it may rain and be warm and muggy. When the cold front arrives there is usually heavy rain, a sudden drop in temperature and an --------- in pressure. Once the depression has passed through the temperature remains ------ the wind is in the ---------- and the forecast is for -------- intervals and scattered --------.

| rain | increase | east | cold | north-west | temperatures |
| west | sunny | pressure | showers | anti-clockwise | Atlantic |

Use Resource K to answer the following questions.
1. What is the date and time of the weather map?
2. What is the temperature in Donaghadee?
3. What is the cloud cover in Dungannon?
4. What is the wind speed and direction in Belleek?
5. As the depression moves east what will happen to the weather in Dungannon?
6. If it takes six hours for the cold front to pass into the Irish Sea, try to give a forecast for Donaghadee for the next twelve hours.

Weather

Anticyclones

In between depressions, the pressure rises and gives us areas of **high** pressure or **anticyclones** and can last anything from a few days to three weeks. They give fine settled weather whatever time of year they happen. The main difference between a summer high and a winter high is the temperature. Look at Resource L. It shows two high-pressure systems over Northern Ireland, one in summer and one in winter.

Resource L ▶

Features of an anticyclone

- High pressure
- Fine settled weather
- Light winds
- Winds blow clockwise
- Often affects the whole of the country
- Summers – hot, sunny, weather with 'heat wave' conditions
- Winters – cold frosty days with fog and icy roads

For Key, see page 39.

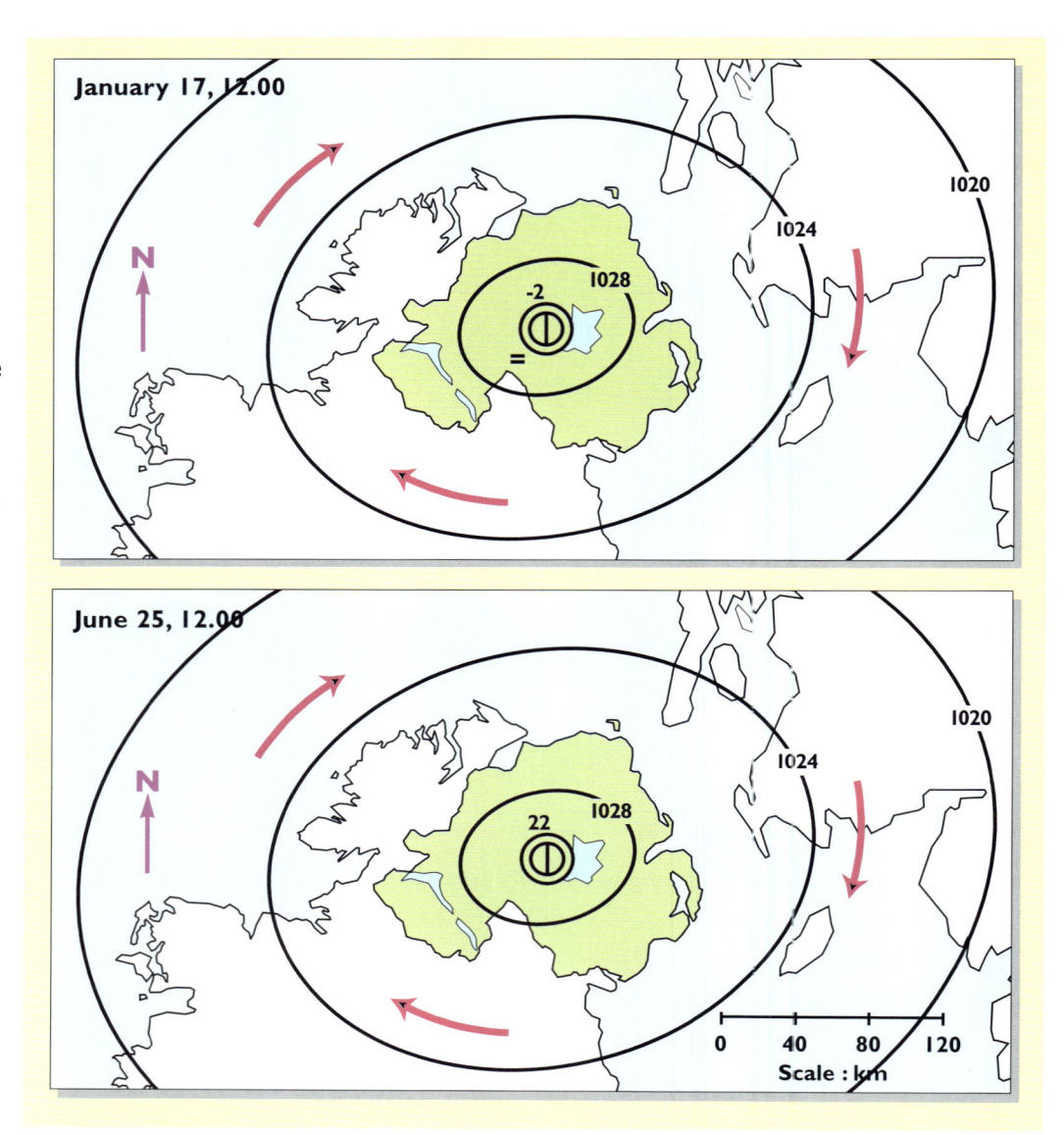

Exercises

Copy and complete the following paragraph using words from the box below:

Anticyclones or ---------- pressure systems can occur at any time of the year and they bring the same sort of conditions. Skies are ------- and there is usually little or no ---------. The wind is ---------- and blows in a --------- direction around the anticyclone. In summer a high gives ---- sunny days with temperatures above ----. In winter temperatures can be at or below -------- with mist and -----. Anticyclones can last for a -------- time and will block depressions from the Atlantic.

| freezing | high | cloud | fog | clockwise |
| clear | light | long | warm | 20°C |

Weather

Extreme weather event

Northern Ireland does not suffer from tornadoes, typhoons and hurricanes. These are confined to tropical areas close to the Equator. Depressions (see pages 38-39) give us stormy weather. Normally these are not destructive but sometimes the pressure is very low and we have gale force winds that cause a lot of damage. On December 26th 1998 a very deep depression hit Northern Ireland. Most people remember it as the Boxing Day storm and everyone had a tale to tell of chimney pots blown down, fences wrecked, trees down, garden sheds demolished and slates off. What exactly happened on Boxing Day and what sort of damage was caused?

The storm was a result of two depressions that blew in from the Atlantic bringing south-westerly winds and heavy rain. The storm affected all of Ireland and then travelled east to devastate parts of northern England and Wales. For nine hours from 3.00pm the wind blew steadily at 50mph and gusts reached over 100mph at Malin Head. The pressure dropped to less than 950 millibars at around 6.00 pm. The winds were very strong. Belfast had over 24 mm of rain in 48 hours. Resource M shows some of the effects of the storm and its aftermath. It was the worst storm there has been in Northern Ireland since 1961.

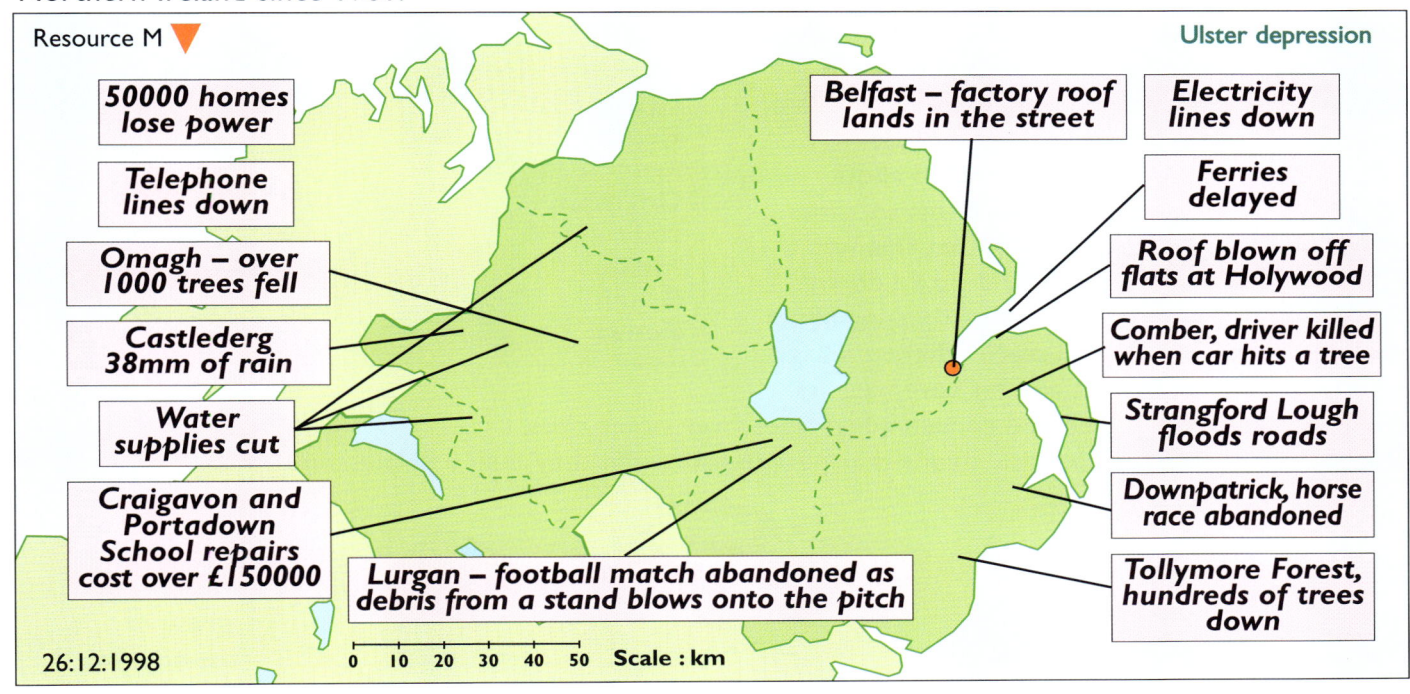

Resource M — Ulster depression

- 50000 homes lose power
- Telephone lines down
- Omagh – over 1000 trees fell
- Castlederg 38mm of rain
- Water supplies cut
- Craigavon and Portadown School repairs cost over £150000
- Lurgan – football match abandoned as debris from a stand blows onto the pitch
- Belfast – factory roof lands in the street
- Electricity lines down
- Ferries delayed
- Roof blown off flats at Holywood
- Comber, driver killed when car hits a tree
- Strangford Lough floods roads
- Downpatrick, horse race abandoned
- Tollymore Forest, hundreds of trees down

26:12:1998 Scale: km 0 10 20 30 40 50

Clearing up was made more difficult by two further storms in the following week. Repairs to over 1000 damaged electricity pylons were made more difficult by near freezing temperatures, strong winds and rain. Some areas were without power for up to a week, while in other areas temporary repairs were damaged and power was lost for a second time. The total cost of the storm to Northern Ireland Electricity was £12 million. This was made up of repair bills, overtime payments and goodwill payments to customers who lost their supply for more than 24 hours.

Tree damage in Tollymore Forest, Co Down.

Settlement

A **settlement** is a place where people live. It can be as small as a group of houses round a cross roads or as large as a big city. In this section we will learn about settlements, why they are there, and why some stay small and others continue to grow. In Northern Ireland 65% of the population live in settlements of more than 1000 people. This may sound quite a lot but it is low compared to the rest of the United Kingdom and other countries in Europe. People who live in settlements live in **urban** areas – towns, villages, cities. People who live in the countryside live in **rural** areas (see Resource A).

Site

We need to ask: why do settlements start? Even a city as big as Belfast started off as one house. It was then joined by other houses because the people who came along decided that this was a good area to live. Try to imagine Patrick O'Caveman wandering round Ireland about 4000 years ago with his club over his shoulder. What made him stop and think that this was a good place to build a house and settle down? Patrick didn't know it but he was thinking about the **site**, that is, the actual place where a village or town grew up. Patrick and his caveman friends picked sites which had certain advantages over other sites. Resource B shows the six basic needs that people had when they built a settlement.

Country	% Urban	% Rural
Northern Ireland	65	35
Great Britain	91	9
Republic of Ireland	57	43
France	75	25
Germany	85	15
Italy	65	35
India	25	75
Brazil	75	25
Kenya	25	75

▲ Resource A

Resource B ▶

- **Fresh water supply** – *usually a river*
- **Arable land to grow crops** – *usually flat*
- **Grazing land for animals** – *can be hilly*
- **Building materials for a house** – *usually wood; this would provide shelter*
- **Fuel for heat and cooking** – *usually wood*
- **Defence against enemies** – *usually a hilltop or some other feature which was easy to defend*

Settlement

Buildings

All settlements have different types of buildings. Houses are the most common type of building in settlements. Other buildings include shops, offices, garages, schools, churches, village halls, clinics, hospitals, leisure centres, factories and many more. The bigger the settlement, the more buildings it will have. A village may have one pub whereas a large town may have twenty or thirty.

List the different types of building around

a) your school

b) your home

Although houses are the most common type of building there are many different types of housing.

Exercises

1. Use the figures in Resource A to draw two pie charts showing urban and rural population in Northern Ireland and one other country.

2. Draw a bar chart to show the urban population for all the countries in the list.

Resource B

3. Identify the different house types in Resource B by matching the number in the photograph to the type of house from the list below

| Bungalow | Semi-detached | Villa | Detached |
| Tower block | Flat | Terrace | Chalet bungalow |

4. Match the beginnings of the sentences on the left with their endings on the right.

In Northern Ireland most people	the actual place where a settlement grows up.
Water supply is	fuel and building.
Early people needed wood for	live in urban areas.
A settlement is	a basic need for settlement.
The site of a settlement is	a place where people live.

5. Try to find out why the settlement where you live grew up where it did. If you live in a rural area, try to find out about a large settlement near you.

Settlement

House types

People live in different house types; which type do you live in? Do a survey for your class and draw a bar chart to show your results.

Copy the table below and say what type of house might be suitable for the families listed. Try to give a reason for your answer.

Resource C ▼

Family	Suitable House	Reason
▶ 2 Adults and 4 children	?	?
▶ Newly married couple – no children	?	?
▶ Single young person aged 18	?	?
▶ Pensioner couple	?	?
▶ Business couple 50+, no children living at home	?	?
▶ Extended family 2 adults, 3 children & 2 grandparents	?	?
▶ Single parent family with 2 children under 5	?	?

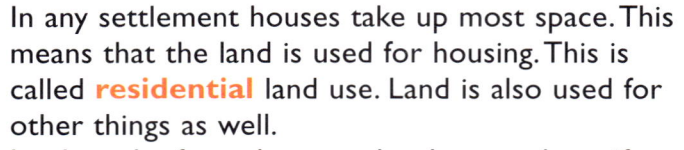

In any settlement houses take up most space. This means that the land is used for housing. This is called **residential** land use. Land is also used for other things as well.

Look at the four photographs above and see if you can match up these different types of land use with the photograph.

A Land used mainly for factories is called **industrial** land use.
B Land used mainly for games and sports is called **recreational** land use.
C Land used for car parks, bus and railway stations is called **transport** land use.
D Land used for shops and offices is called **commercial** land use.

44

Settlement

Settlement hierarchy

Settlements are divided by size and the services they offer. Resource D shows one possible order of settlements for Northern Ireland. In other bigger countries this order would be different. In the USA a settlement of 8000 people would be far too small to be called a town, but in Northern Ireland it *would* be a town.

Resource D ▼

Settlement type	Size	Description
Hamlet	less than 100	houses only, no services.
Village	less than 2 000	at least a shop, pub, church and a primary school
Small town	less than 20 000	more shops, pubs, churches and possibly a high school and a bank
Large Town	less than 100 000	everything above, + a library, fire station, police station, and several high schools.
City	100 000 +	everything above + a university, cathedral, chain stores and headquarters of organisations

This arrangement is called a **hierarchy** – putting settlements in order according to their size. Resource E shows what happens in Northern Ireland.

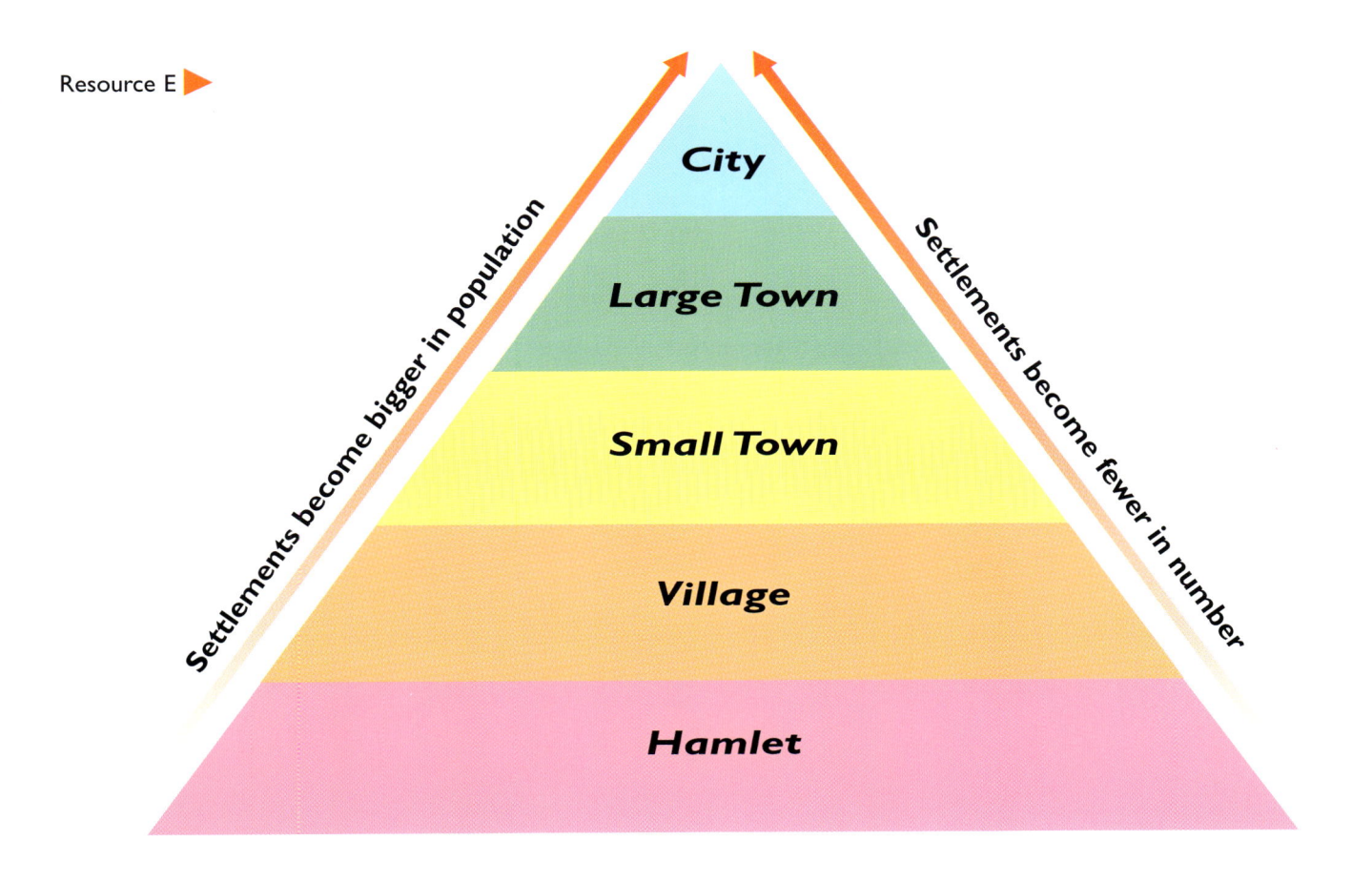

Resource E ▶

Settlements become bigger in population

City
Large Town
Small Town
Village
Hamlet

Settlements become fewer in number

Settlement

Settlement size in Northern Ireland

Use the following table of settlement sizes to decide how many cities, large towns and small towns there are in Northern Ireland.

Source: 1991 NI Census

Settlement	Population	Settlement	Population
Greater Belfast*	360 000	Armagh	15 000
Derry/Londonderry	73 000	Banbridge	12 000
Bangor	53 000	Enniskillen	12 000
Lisburn	42 000	Strabane	12 000
Ballymena	29 000	Downpatrick	11 000
Newtownards	24 000	Limavady	11 000
Carrickfergus	23 000	Cookstown	10 000
Newry	22 000	Craigavon+	10 000
Lurgan+	22 000	Dungannon	10 000
Portadown+	22 000	Holywood	10 000
Antrim	21 000	Comber	9 000
Coleraine	21 000	Ballyclare	8 000
Larne	18 000	Newcastle	8 000
Omagh	18 000	Ballymoney	8 000

* Greater Belfast includes Newtownabbey, Dundonald and Dunmurry.
Craigavon, Portadown and Lurgan combine to give a population of 54,000.

Resource F

Use the Northern Ireland map on page 4 to find out how many settlements mentioned in Resource F are in each of the six counties.

If you live in or near one of these settlements you might find yourself disagreeing with the answers.
According to the population, Derry is a large town but when you look at the services it provides most people would agree that it is a city. The boundary line between small towns and villages is also arguable. Look at the list of counties below in Resource G. In each case there are two settlements with their populations. One is more than 2000 and should be a small town while the other is less than 2000 and is classed as a village. If you live in or near these settlements you might disagree. Sometimes you need to know the population and the services to decide, and your teacher might ask you to do a survey of the services in a settlement near you! Once you know how many shops, schools, pubs and churches a settlement has – and if you know the population – then it is easier to decide.

Resource G

County	Small town?	Village?
Antrim	Ballycastle (4000)	Bushmills (1400)
Armagh	Richill (2800)	Markethill (1400)
Down	Ballynahinch (4600)	Crossgar (1300)
Fermanagh	Lisnaskea (2400)	Irvinestown (1900)
Londonderry	Dungiven (2900)	Kilrea (1300)
Tyrone	Coalisland (3800)	Fivemiletown (1100)

Source: 1991 NI Census.

Settlement

Case Study: Settlement on the Ards Peninsula

Here are some of the smaller settlements on the Ards Peninsula. Study their populations and services and decide which are hamlets, which are villages and which are small towns. If you live in the area you might like to discuss your findings, or visit some of the settlements to see what you think. If you live elsewhere, make a list of settlements in your area which could be studied by your school in a similar way.

Settlement	Population	Bread Shop		Newsagent		Primary Schools		Churches		Clothes Shop	
Ballyhalbert	270	2	1	1	1	1	1	1	1	0	0
Ballywalter	1100	5	1	4	2	1	1	2	2	1	1
Carrowdore	360	2	2	1	1	1	1	1	1	0	0
Cloughy	500	2	2	1	2	1	1	1	1	0	0
Donaghadee	4500	10	6	7	4	2	2	6	6	5	4
Greyabbey	750	3	3	1	2	1	1	2	2	0	0
Kircubbin	1100	6	3	3	3	2	2	3	3	1	1
Millisle	1500	5	4	3	3	1	1	4	4	1	1
Portaferry	2300	8	5	5	3	3	3	5	5	1	1
Portavogie	1500	4	2	3	1	1	1	2	2	0	0

Resource H ▲

Population source: 1991 NI Census
1993 figures in green
1999 figures in red.

Scrabo Tower, on Scrabo Hill, outside Newtownards. This sandstone monument is a landmark at the north end of the Ards Peninsula.

Exercises

Draw a scattergraph to show the population plotted against the number of services.
Your population scale could go from 0 to 4500, while your services scale could go from 0 to 30.
Once you have the graph drawn put in a trend line or best fit line. This is a straight line which goes through or near as many points as possible. Then answer the following questions:

1. Is the graph positive or negative?

2. Are any of the settlements way off line? If so can you say why?

3. Comment on the relationship between the size of the settlement and the number of services it provides.

4. If you were to open a clothes shop would you be better to open it in **Donaghadee** or in **Portavogie**? Discuss this with your class and give reasons for your answer before taking a vote.

5. Use the map of Northern Ireland on page 4 to say where the people of the Ards Peninsula might shop for shoes, jewellery or books.

6. Population in these settlements is growing, so why are there fewer services in 1999 than in 1993?

Settlement

High and low order shops

Shops and settlements go together, the bigger the settlement the more shops it will have. More people attract more shops and more shops encourage more people to live there. This is called **the spiral of growth**. There are different types of shops however; some of them we use frequently while others we use very rarely. By looking at the type of shops in a settlement it is easier to decide whereabouts in the hierarchy it will go. Shops can be divided as follows:

1 Low order shops
These are shops which we use on a regular basis, perhaps daily or weekly. They include supermarkets, newsagents, confectioners, bakers and butchers. We spend relatively small amounts and only travel a short distance to get there. If you call at a shop for crisps or chocolate on the way to school every day this is a good example of low order shopping. Someone buying a paper on the way to work or a loaf of bread on the way home would also be low order shopping. These are called convenience goods. Villages normally have low order shops.

2 High order shops
These are shops which we use now and again, perhaps once a year or even less. They include car showrooms, furniture shops, electrical goods, estate agents and undertakers! We may spend quite a lot of money when we are there and may be prepared to travel a long distance to get there. Items we buy are sometimes called comparison goods because we will compare makes and prices before we buy. A new car or a new carpet are good examples – people may visit as many as ten shops before buying. High order shops are more common in towns and cities.

3 Shops selling goods
These can be high or low order and you normally take the item with you or arrange delivery if it is too big to carry. Goods include newsagents, bakers, supermarkets, carpet shops and clothes shops.

4 Shops selling services
These can also be low or high order but the shop provides a service at a price. A rough rule of thumb is that a service is something you can do yourself but it is easier or more convenient to pay someone to do it for you. Estate agents, hairdressers, take-aways, insurance brokers and undertakers are good examples of services.

5 Shops selling goods and services
Some shops cannot fit easily into the four types outlined above. The Post Office provides goods and services, as do garages which sell petrol and repair cars.
Chemists also provide both. Obviously they sell goods, but what service do they provide?

48

Settlement

Exercises

Draw a large copy of the matrix below and try to put the following shops into the correct columns:

newsagent	**estate agent**	**café**	**Tesco**	**optician**	**clothes shop**
car showroom	**Spar**	**greengrocer**	**carpet shop**	**shoe shop**	**butcher**
hairdresser	**pub**	**bank**	**florist**	**travel agent**	**book shop**

Be prepared to argue your point of view and don't assume that your teacher always has the right answers. Sometimes more than one answer might be right!

	Goods	Both	Services
High Order			
Low Order			

Some shops do not fit easily into any of the above boxes. There are different reasons for this. The shop may be used a lot by some people and never by others, eg a bookmaker. The shop might be visited once a month or six weeks and it is difficult to say whether it is high or low order, eg a chemist.

Look at the shops pictured below and decide which box they might go in – or do you need a new box?

Discuss in groups and with your teacher and see if you can come up with an answer to this. Remember you might have to agree to disagree!

Settlement

Urban zones

Cities like Belfast will have many large areas of housing and a smaller number of industrial areas. Villages like Bellaghy may have no industrial areas at all. Sometimes these land use areas form a pattern, although usually this happens only in cities and large towns. The simplest pattern is circular with the oldest buildings in the centre and the newest round the outside. Resource 1 shows a simple pattern.

Resource 1 ▶

A B C D E

Zone A — **The commercial zone.** This has shops, offices, banks, department stores and multi-storey car parks. There are very few houses in this zone.

Zone B — **The inner city zone.** This is an area of older houses, usually terraced with no gardens and little open space. Many of the houses will have been modernised or re-developed.

Zone C — **The inner suburbs.** These are made up of houses built between 1920 and 1950. They are usually red brick semi-detached. They have gardens and more open space.

Zone D — **The outer suburbs.** These are newer estates often with detached houses and bungalows. They have been built since 1960 and contain industrial estates as well as Housing Executive estates.

Zone E — **The Green Belt.** This is an area of land round the city or town to stop it growing any bigger. It is composed of farmland and leisure facilities like parks, golf courses and sports pitches. Development is strictly controlled.

Exercises

Look at the sentences written below and write out the five which are true

The oldest buildings are in Zone A.
The Green Belt contains large areas of housing.
Industrial estates are found in Zone E.
Zone B contains little open space.
The inner suburbs were built in 1980.
Bungalows are common in Zone D.
Zone A is mainly shops and offices.
Golf courses are allowed in the Green Belt.

Settlement

Site

If the site was a good one, then other houses would be built and the settlement would develop into a village. If the site was especially good, it would attract enemies who might like to take it over for themselves, so a castle might be built. This in turn would attract shops to supply the castle and the houses and this would attract more houses, so the settlement would grow bigger. The pictures below show other features which become important as settlements grow bigger. (The sketch maps are not to scale!)

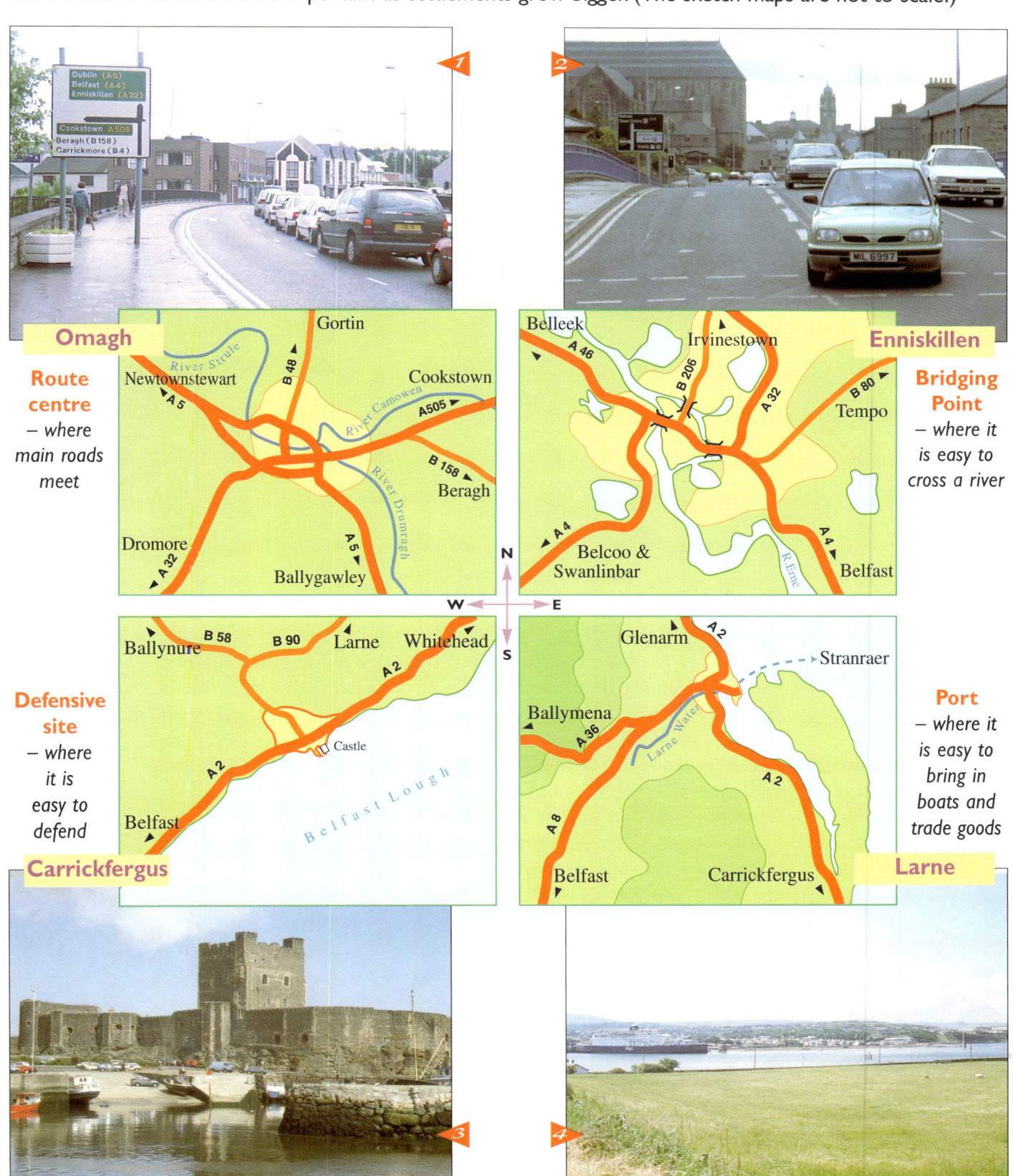

Omagh

Route centre – where main roads meet

Enniskillen

Bridging Point – where it is easy to cross a river

Defensive site – where it is easy to defend

Carrickfergus

Port – where it is easy to bring in boats and trade goods

Larne

Settlement

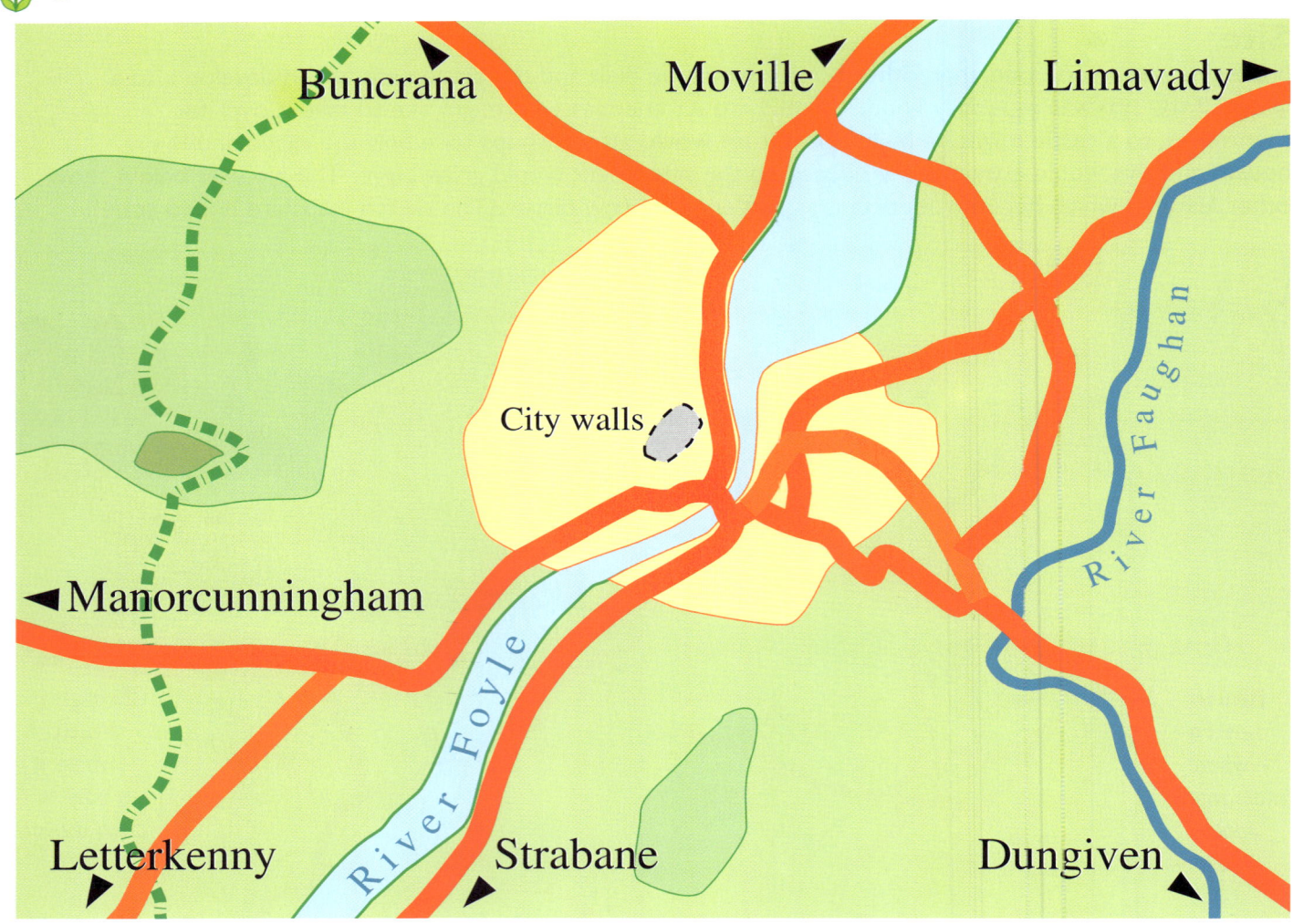

Sketch map – Site of Derry

Derry/Londonderry is a very good example of a site which provided many of the features needed for settlement and growth. It had everything that Patrick O'Caveman was looking for when it was founded over 1100 years ago.

- Fresh water supplies – *from streams flowing into the River Foyle.*
- Arable land to grow crops – *downstream on each side of the river.*
- Grazing land for animals – *east and west of the river.*
- Building materials for a house – *Derry means 'oak grove' in Gaelic.*
- Fuel for heat and cooking – *the same oak trees used for building.*
- Defence against enemies – *the famous walls of Derry.*

If you look at the map you will see that it was also:

- **A port** – ships could sail up the Foyle and dock near the town.
- **A bridging point** – in fact the lowest bridging point on the Foyle.
- **A route centre** – linking Londonderry and Donegal.

Settement

Exercises

Look at the map on page 8. There are two main settlements shown on it, Bushmills (9440) and Portballintrae (9241).

There are also a number of smaller settlements, Ballyallaght (9642), Derrykeighan (9633), Castlecat (9537), Billy (9538), Liscolman (9836) and Lisnagunogue (9742).

Copy and complete the following table showing the services that each provides and then try to decide where they would fit on the settlement hierarchy: small town, village or hamlet. Shops are not shown on the map, so column 6 gives you the total numbers of all high and low order shops.

	1	2	3	4	5	6
Bushmills						56
Portballintrae						2
Ballyallaght						0
Derrykeighan						1
Castlecat						0
Billy						0
Liscolman						1
Lisnagunogue						1

1 = Number of main/ Class A roads
2 = Number of churches
3 = Number of Post Offices/telephones
4 = Number of schools
5 = Number of other services
6 = Number of shops

View of Derry city, looking towards The Diamond

Interesting Fact

The largest towns in the Republic of Ireland are:

Greater Dublin	950000 +
Cork	180000
Limerick	79000
Galway	57000
Waterford	44000

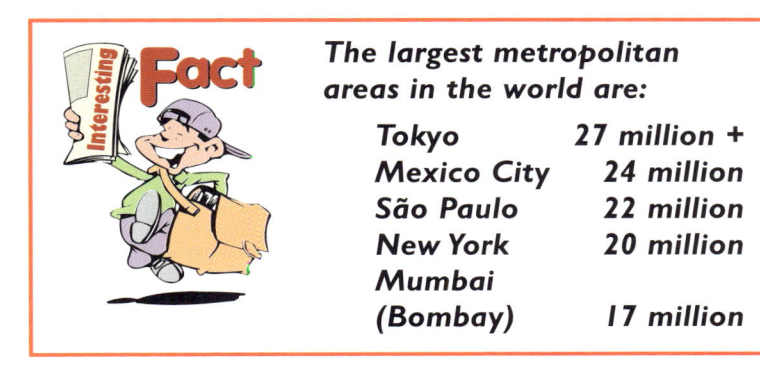

Interesting Fact

The largest metropolitan areas in the world are:

Tokyo	27 million +
Mexico City	24 million
São Paulo	22 million
New York	20 million
Mumbai (Bombay)	17 million

Population

Population is the number of people who live in an area. Some areas have many people while other areas have very few. Some areas of the world, such as the Arctic and Antarctic, are nearly empty of people. Large cities like London and New York have many people. Areas with many people are **densely populated**, while areas with very few people are **sparsely populated**. Northern Ireland is somewhere in between, but there are areas with very few people eg the Mourne Mountains. There are also areas with many people, eg large settlements like Belfast or Derry.

Population

The population of Northern Ireland is around 1 600 000 or 1.6 million. Resource A shows the population of the countries which make up the British Isles.

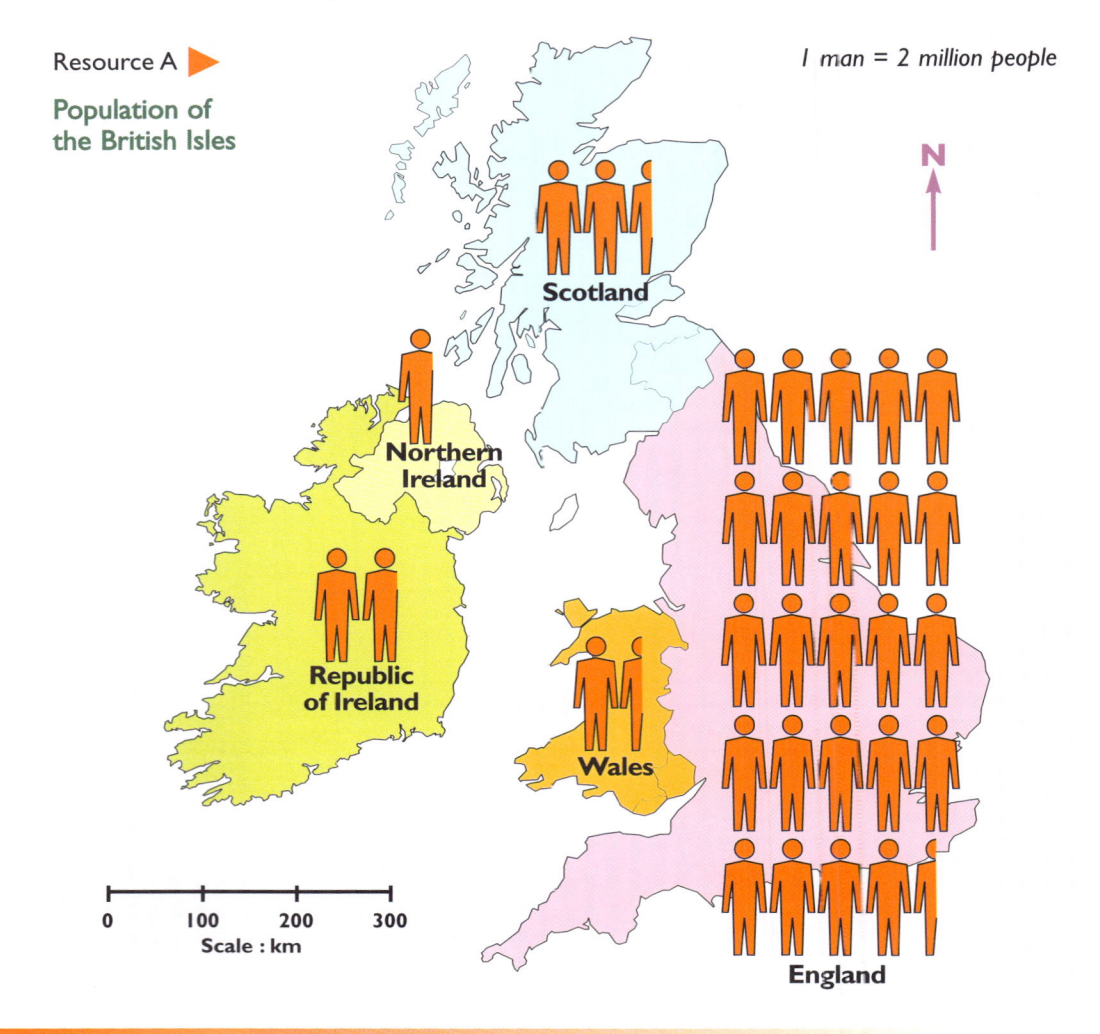

Resource A ▶
Population of the British Isles

1 man = 2 million people

Exercises

a) Draw a bar chart to show the population of the five countries.
b) Copy and complete the following table into your notebook. You may need an atlas to help you.

Country	Capital	Population
England	L_____	_____ million
Scotland	E_____	_____ million
Republic of Ireland	D_____	_____ million
Wales	C_____	_____ million
Northern Ireland	B_____	_____ million

Population

Northern Ireland is part of the UK. The UK is part of the European Union. The European Union is made up of 15 countries whose total population is 373.1 million. On a European scale Northern Ireland becomes a very small country indeed. Resource B shows the population figures for the fifteen countries of the European Union.

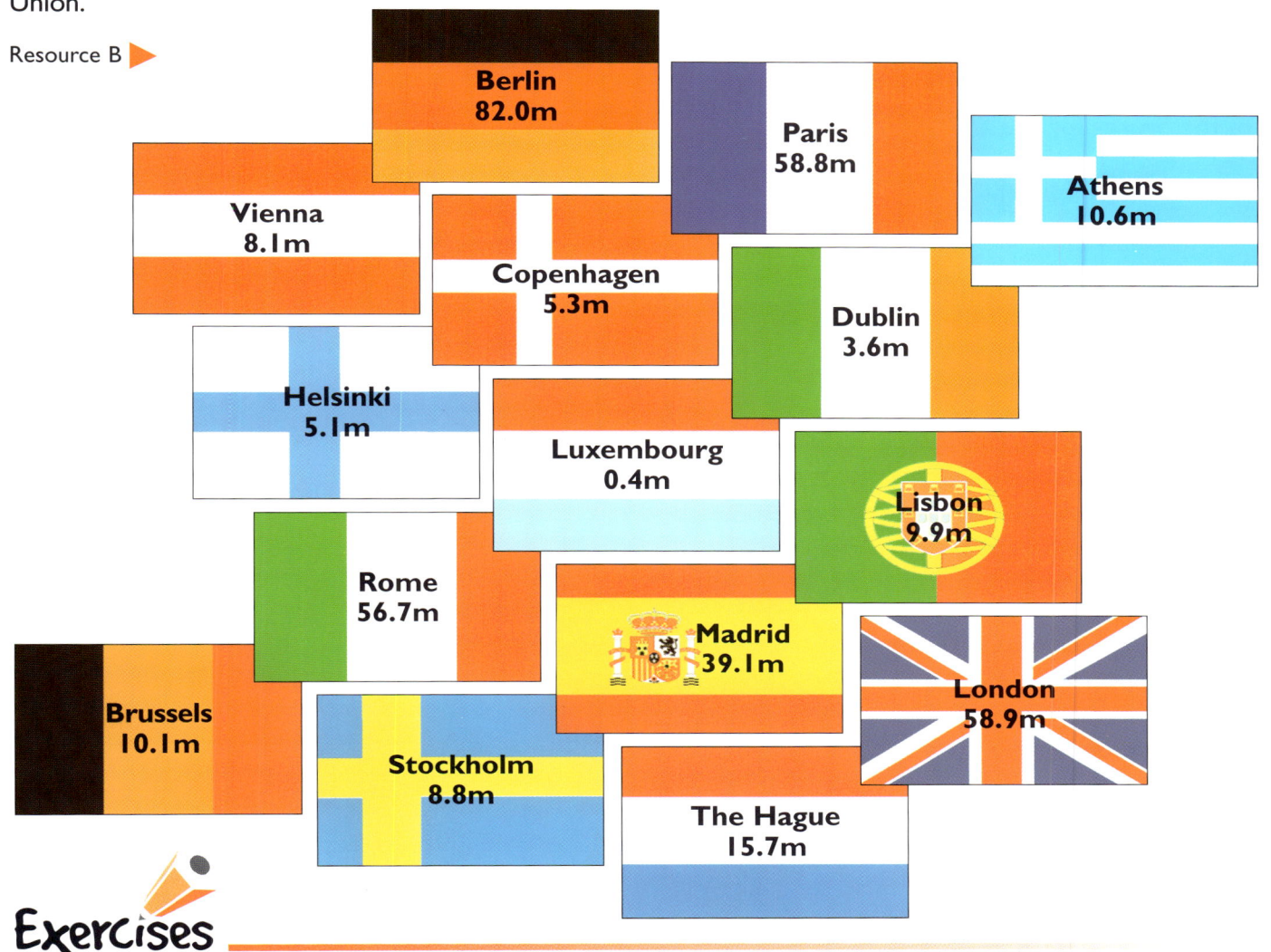

Resource B ▶

- Berlin 82.0m
- Paris 58.8m
- Athens 10.6m
- Vienna 8.1m
- Copenhagen 5.3m
- Dublin 3.6m
- Helsinki 5.1m
- Luxembourg 0.4m
- Lisbon 9.9m
- Rome 56.7m
- Madrid 39.1m
- London 58.9m
- Brussels 10.1m
- Stockholm 8.8m
- The Hague 15.7m

Exercises

Using the flag and/or the capital try to name the fifteen countries in the European Union.

Even the UK is small when compared to other countries. Resource C shows the population of countries we looked at on page 42 when we were looking at rural and urban population. It also shows the **population density** of these countries. This will be referred to on page 56.

Resource C ▶

Country	Population (millions)	Population density (per square km)
United Kingdom (including NI)	59 m	241
Republic of Ireland	3.6 m	51
France	59m	108
Germany	82m	230
Italy	57m	189
India	1000m	299
Brazil	170m	20
Kenya	28m	48

55

Population

Population density

Resource C shows the countries of the European Union but we have no idea of the size of the country compared to the population. The UK and France have almost the same population but if you look at a map you will see that France is much bigger than the UK. If we divide the population of the country by the area this will tell us on average how many people there are in each square kilometre. This is called the **population density**. Population density is always given per square kilometre – **psk** for short. Here are the figures for the UK and France.

Country	Population (m)	Area (sq. km)	Density (psk)
UK	58.9	244820	241
France	58.8	547030	108

The UK is more densely populated than France. This means that on average there are more people per square km in the UK than there are in France. One square km in France has 108 people living in it while in the UK there would be 241 people living in the same area.

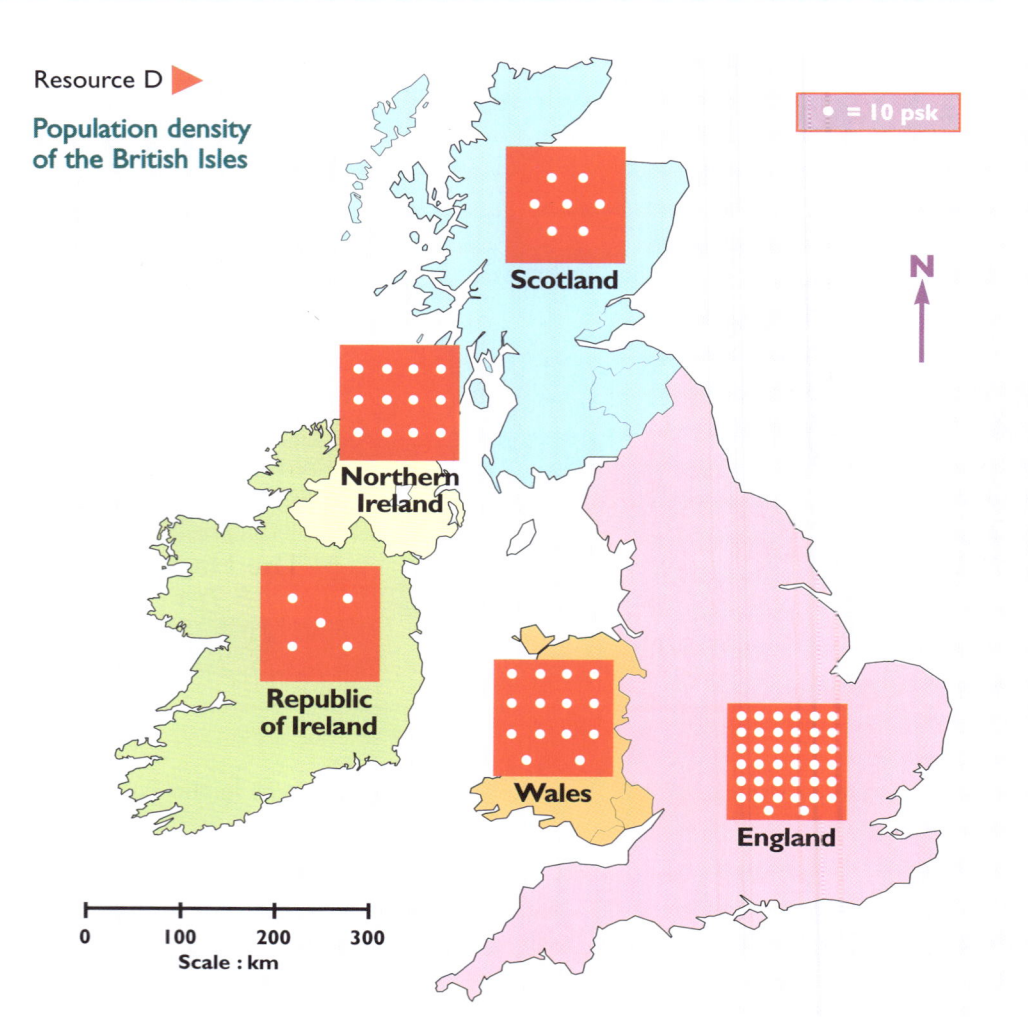

Resource D

Population density of the British Isles

• = 10 psk

Resource D shows the population density for the five countries of the British Isles using a scale of one dot for every ten people per square km.

From this we can see that Northern Ireland has a moderate population density. It is not densely populated like England, and it is not sparsely populated like Australia (2psk). If you look back to Resource C you will see the population densities of other countries and you can compare them to Northern Ireland (118psk).

Up-to-date population statistics can be obtained on the Internet. Especially good are: http://www.odci.gov/cia/publications/factbook/index.html and http://www.atlapedia.com/

Why is population density different in different places?

The number of people living in an area depends on a whole range of factors. A sparsely populated area with very few people has a lot of negative factors. A densely populated area with many people has a lot of positive factors. Look at the three photographs below which show three areas of Northern Ireland.

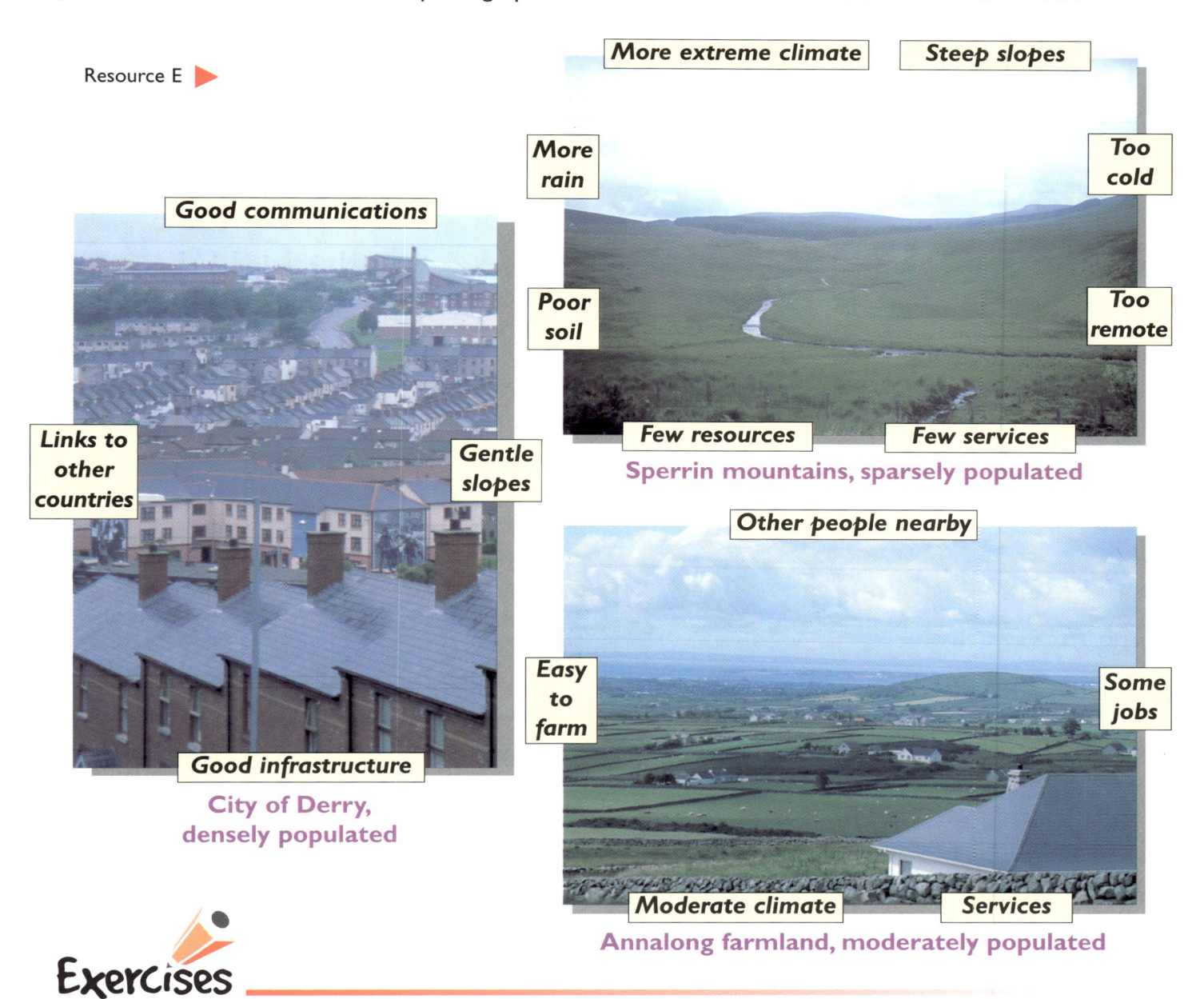

Resource E ▶

Sperrin mountains, sparsely populated
- More extreme climate
- Steep slopes
- More rain
- Too cold
- Poor soil
- Too remote
- Few resources
- Few services

City of Derry, densely populated
- Good communications
- Links to other countries
- Gentle slopes
- Good infrastructure

Annalong farmland, moderately populated
- Other people nearby
- Easy to farm
- Some jobs
- Moderate climate
- Services

Exercises

Make a copy of Resource F in your book. Copy the information from the photographs onto your table. Twelve factors have been left out of the photographs and will need to be added in to your table. They are in the word list below.

Resource F ▶

Sperrin Mountains	Annalong Farmland	City of Derry
Sparsely populated	Moderately populated	Densely populated

Difficult to farm — Flat land — Good standard of living — Close to services
Few jobs — Good soils — Many industries — Little industry
Strong winds — Many jobs — Good road links — Wide choice of services

Population

Look at Resource G which shows Northern Ireland. This is a **choropleth** (colour coded) map showing the population density.

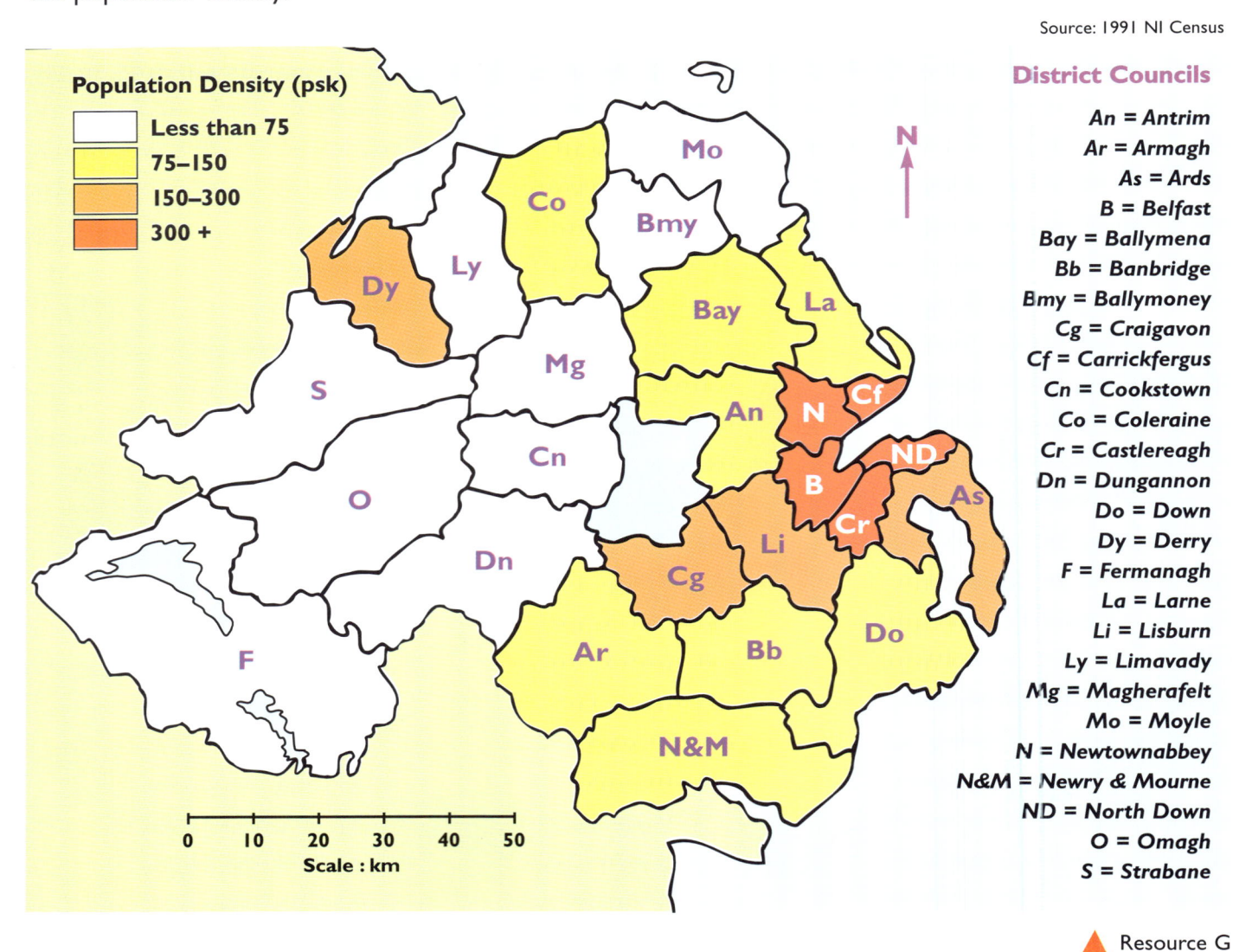

Source: 1991 NI Census

Population Density (psk)
- Less than 75
- 75–150
- 150–300
- 300 +

District Councils

An = Antrim
Ar = Armagh
As = Ards
B = Belfast
Bay = Ballymena
Bb = Banbridge
Bmy = Ballymoney
Cg = Craigavon
Cf = Carrickfergus
Cn = Cookstown
Co = Coleraine
Cr = Castlereagh
Dn = Dungannon
Do = Down
Dy = Derry
F = Fermanagh
La = Larne
Li = Lisburn
Ly = Limavady
Mg = Magherafelt
Mo = Moyle
N = Newtownabbey
N&M = Newry & Mourne
ND = North Down
O = Omagh
S = Strabane

▲ Resource G

Exercises

1. What is the population density of Strabane District Council area?
2. What is the population density of Castlereagh District Council area?
3. Complete the following sentence using two of the phrases below:
   Population density in Northern Ireland .... and ....
   - … shows no particular pattern
   - … increases from west to east
   - … decreases from west to east
   - … increases as you go north
   - … is lowest around Belfast
   - … is highest around Belfast
4. Using the maps on pages 23, 34 and 35 try to give reasons why there are lower population densities in counties Fermanagh, Tyrone and Londonderry.

Population

Changes in population

Population does not always stay the same. There are three factors that change a population.

Birth rate	Death rate	Migration
The number of babies born per 1000 people per year	The number of people who die per 1000 people per year	The number of people who move into or out of an area

There are usually more births than deaths. If you subtract the number of deaths from the number of births you have the **growth rate** or rate of natural increase. So that these figures can be compared they are usually given per thousand (‰). A birth rate of 15 per thousand means that for every thousand people in the country 15 babies are born. Here are recent figures for Northern Ireland.

The Population is 1600000.
The **birth rate** is 15 per thousand, so there are 15 babies born for every thousand people.
15 X 1600 = 24000 babies born in one year.

The **death rate** is 9 per thousand, so there are 9 deaths for every thousand people.
9 X 1600 = 14400 deaths in one year.

The **growth rate** is 6 per thousand, so the population will increase by 6 for every thousand people
6 X 1600 = 9600

The new population is 1609600 — *not counting migration!*

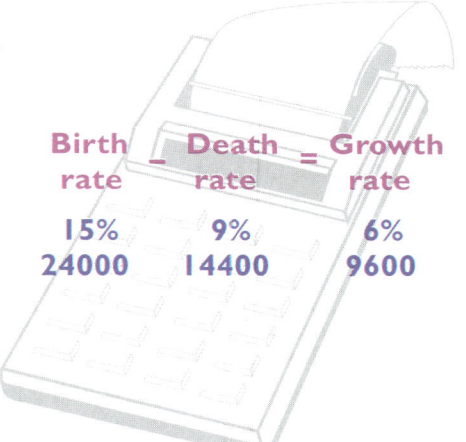

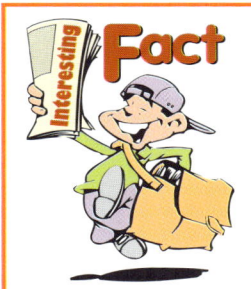

Birth rate	–	Death rate	=	Growth rate
15‰		9‰		6‰
24000		14400		9600

Interesting Fact

In Northern Ireland 24000 babies are born every year; that is roughly:
  2000 per month
  500 per week
  70 per day
  between 2 and 3 every hour.
In the time you spend at school today around 20 babies will be born in Northern Ireland.

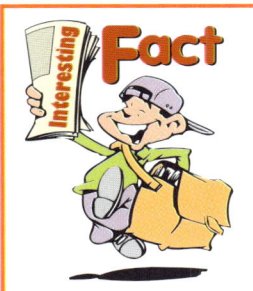

Interesting Fact

World figures are even higher. Every second five babies are born and two people die so the population is increasing by three per second, which is roughly:
  180 per minute
  10800 per hour
  259200 per day
You can work the rest out for yourselves, but it is a lot of people. The UN reckons that the world population reached six billion on 19 July 1999.

Population

Resource H shows the birth, death and growth rates for the countries we have looked at in other chapters.

Country	‰ Birth rate	‰ Death rate	‰ Growth rate
Northern Ireland	15	9	6
Republic of Ireland	??	9	4
Great Britain	12	?	1
France	12	9	?
Germany	9	11	-2
Italy	9	10	-?
India	26	?	17
Brazil	??	9	12
Kenya	32	14	?

◀ Resource H

Exercises

Copy and complete the table, then answer these questions:
1 Which country has the highest birth rate?
2 Which country is growing fastest?
3 Which country would seem to have the worst health care?
4 Name two **More Economically Developed Countries (MEDC)**.
5 Name two **Less Economically Developed Countries (LEDC)**.
6 What is happening to the population in Germany and Italy?
7 Germany's population is, in fact, still rising. How can this happen?

If you answered question 7 correctly, you will have realised that migration also affects the population of a country. There are different types of migration:

Local migration	**Regional migration**	**International migration**
from one street in a town to another	from one part of the country to another	from one country to another

Migration can also be **forced** or **voluntary**.

Exercises

Look at the following situations and say which type of migration they are. Imagine that these changes are taking place in the settlement where you live, or in a nearby settlement.
1 Old age pensioners moving to a smaller house in the town.
2 A teenager moving to London to look for work.
3 A young couple going to Australia to join relatives.
4 A family moving to another town because of sectarian intimidation.
5 A man moving to Dublin because his firm has opened a new business there and he has been transferred to it.
6 A family of five moving to a larger house in the same town.
7 A family moving from Hong Kong to Northern Ireland to open a restaurant.

Population

Look at Resource I, which shows the population of Northern Ireland from 1821. Many of the changes in population over the years can be explained by migration rather than by changes in birth and death rates.

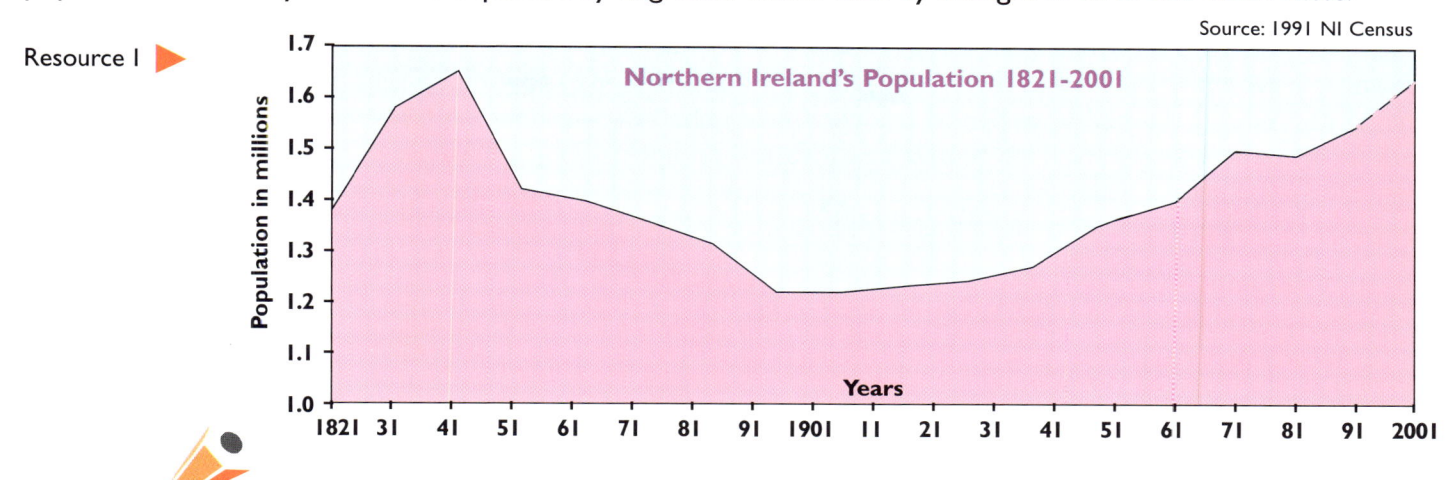

Resource I ▶

Northern Ireland's Population 1821-2001

Source: 1991 NI Census

Exercises

1. What was the population in 1821?
2. In which year was the population highest?
3. What might have caused the sudden drop in population between 1841 and 1851?
4. Why did the population continue to decline in the late nineteenth century?
5. What might have caused the slight dip in population between 1971 and 1981?

Resource I shows the changes over a number of years. Resource J shows us that changes can also take place over a small period of time. The map shows the percentage change in population from 1981 to 1991 in the local government districts in Northern Ireland. Birth and death rates can explain some of these, but other changes are a result of migration.
The key to District Council names is on Resource G, page 58.

Resource J ▶

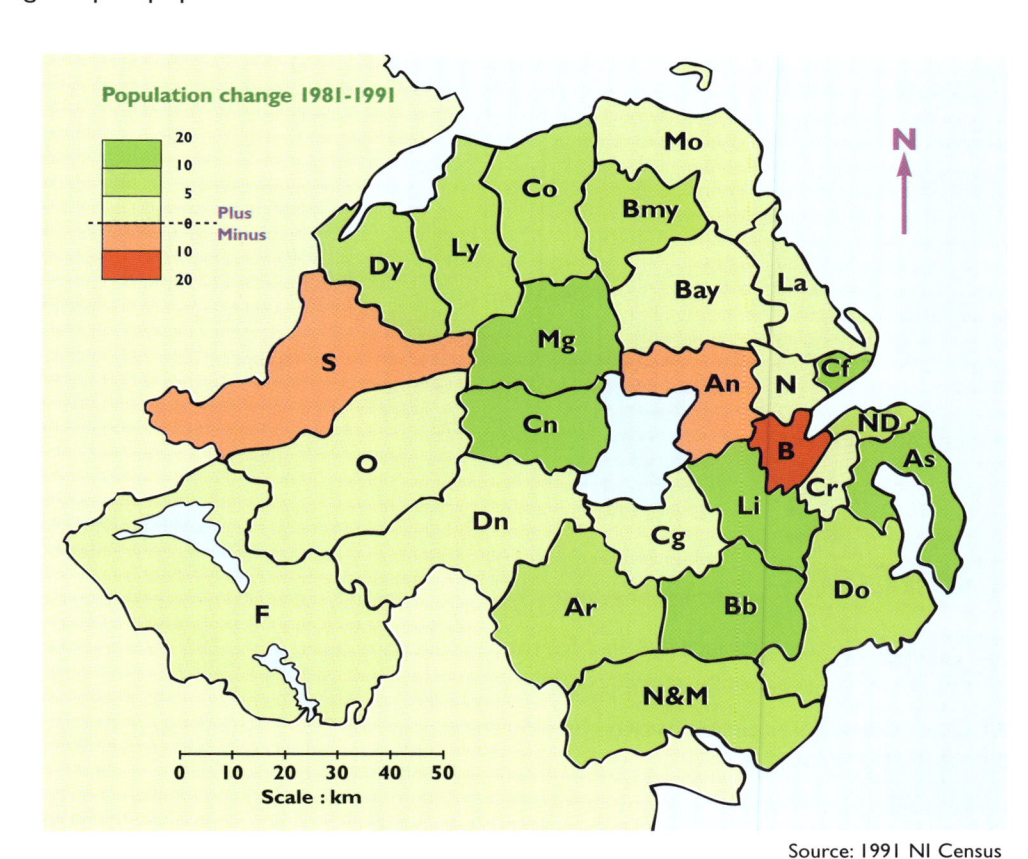

Source: 1991 NI Census

Exercises

1. What is the percentage increase or decrease in Moyle, Strabane and Banbridge?
2. Name two areas that have increased by more than 10%.
3. State the area which has decreased by the greatest amount, and give one reason why you think this has happened.

Population

Population Composition

We need to know how many people a country has if we are to provide the services that people need. Northern Ireland has 1.6 million people. How much electricity is needed, how many houses, how much food or how many reservoirs for water? We also need to know how many schools to build or how many retirement homes? In order to answer these questions we need to know how many people there are in different age groups. This is called population composition – a breakdown of the population by age and sex – this is called an **age-sex pyramid** or **population pyramid**. Resource K shows three population pyramids, one for Northern Ireland, one for Belfast and one for Fermanagh.

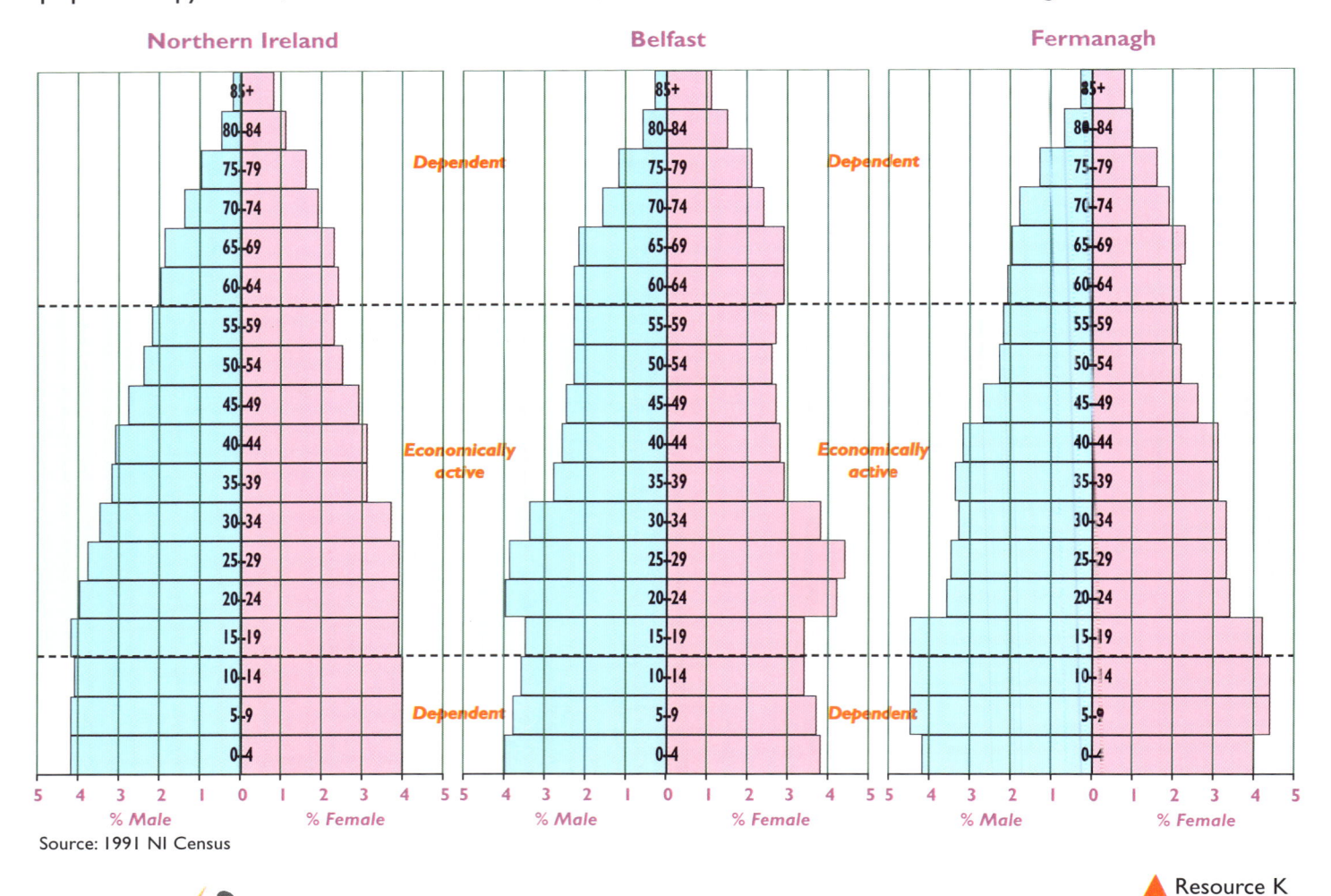

Source: 1991 NI Census

Resource K

Exercises

a) What percentage of females in Northern Ireland is aged 25 - 29?

b) What percentage of Belfast's population is aged 0 - 4?

c) Give two differences between the population pyramids of Belfast and Fermanagh.

d) Try and give reasons for the differences outlined in (c).

e) Look at the 0 - 4 age group in Fermanagh compared to the 5 - 19 age groups. What does this tell you about the birth rate in the county?

f) What plans might need to be made regarding primary school places as a result of this?

g) Look at the 85+ age group for Northern Ireland. Can you say why there are four times as many women as men?

h) In the light of this imbalance in the population, what might planners need to think about if they are planning facilities for the 85+ age group in future years?

Age and sex divide each pyramid, but it also divides the population into three age groups:

Under 15	These are part of the **dependent population**; they do not work and rely on others to support them.
15 – 59	These are the **economically active** part of the population; they work and pay taxes and insurance which helps to support the dependents.
60 +	These are also part of the dependent population as they are retired and depend on others to support them.

The dependency ratio shows the number of dependents related to the numbers who are economically active. In Northern Ireland the figures are as follows:

Under 15	24.5%	386570
15– 59	58.3%	919876
60 +	17.2%	271390

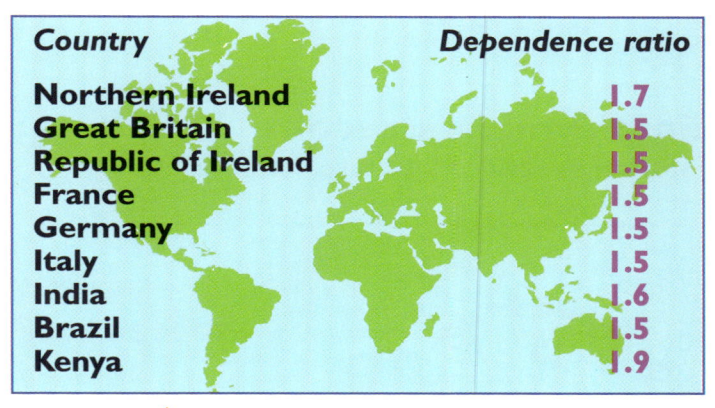

Country	Dependence ratio
Northern Ireland	1.7
Great Britain	1.5
Republic of Ireland	1.5
France	1.5
Germany	1.5
Italy	1.5
India	1.6
Brazil	1.5
Kenya	1.9

Resource L

The dependency ratio is the total population divided by the economically active giving a dependency ratio of 1:1.7. This means that Northern Ireland has one person working for every 1.7 people in the population. This can be compared with the other countries with which we have compared Northern Ireland in previous chapters.

Exercises

Migration

James is about 20 years old. He is able-bodied but was not a high flyer at school. He has just completed his college course and has to make a decision ....

1. Look at the statements on the right.

   Sort them into two groups:
   (i) those that are likely to make James move away from the area (write these out in order of importance).
   (ii) those that are likely to make James stay (write these out in order of importance).

2. What do you think James should do?

   Explain your decision.

3. Imagine that a number of people like James move away from the Belleek area. What would be the consequences
   (i) to Belleek, and
   (ii) to the areas they migrated to?

- James lives in Belleek, Co Fermanagh.
- He has five uncles, three grandparents and a Godfather.
- You cannot beat those peaceful sunsets over the mountains.
- James is a qualified car mechanic and can work on marine engines.
- There is a shortage of part-time work for the active population in Belleek.
- James' girlfriend in Manchester can afford the latest fashions.
- Lakeland holidays are being heavily marketed now.
- James lives with his Grandfather who is 76 years old.
- James met a young woman at College. She works in Manchester these days.
- Fifteen of James' cousins live in Fermanagh. James loves big family get-togethers!
- English people are not quite the same somehow.
- Grandpa's house is large but old-fashioned.
- There is a primary school in Belleek.
- Fermanagh is better off as a result of EU money and grants for tourism.
- James is very fit and enjoys walking around the lakes in Fermanagh.
- Many people in Belleek are over 55 years old.

Economic activity

Economic activity refers to the different ways that people make a living. It is concerned with the jobs they do and how these jobs are linked to one another. Years ago people learned a job or a trade and everyone knew what they did. A potter made pots, a tanner worked with leather, a blacksmith shod horses. Many people were farmers, and if they needed a pot they exchanged some food they had grown for the pot they needed. Today things are much more complicated; there is a wide range of jobs which all depend on one another.

Employment structure
Jobs can be divided into three main types:

Primary
These jobs obtain the raw materials or resources which we need eg farmer, forester, miner.

Secondary
These jobs take the raw material and make it into something useful eg car worker, steel worker.

Tertiary
These jobs provide a service for other people eg teacher, doctor, fireman.

Exercises

Draw three columns in your book titled **Primary**, **Secondary**, and **Tertiary**. Put the following jobs/activities into the correct column:

policeman	quarryman	pop star	BT engineer
home help	car assembly worker	fisherman	mechanic
Cool FM DJ	frozen food factory worker	professional footballer	fitter
lawyer	farmer	TV weatherman	shepherd
shipbuilder	traffic warden	oil rig driller	security guard
forester	soldier	carpet factory worker	

Do a survey in your class to find out which jobs people living at home do. You can record the results on a pie chart.

Economic activity

Compare your figures with the following pie charts for the countries named. How close is your class to the Northern Ireland figures?

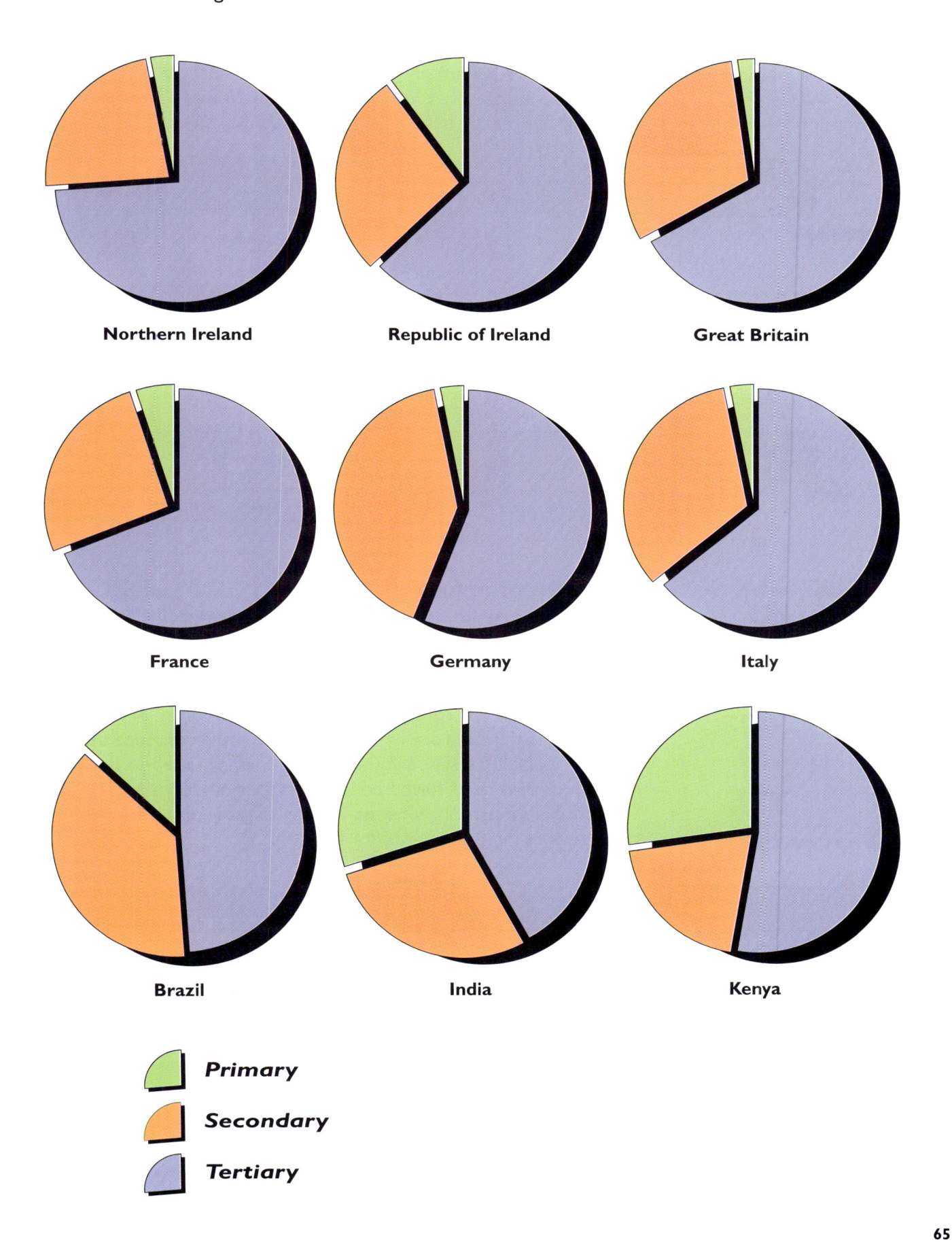

Northern Ireland **Republic of Ireland** **Great Britain**

France **Germany** **Italy**

Brazil **India** **Kenya**

Primary

Secondary

Tertiary

Economic activity

Primary Industry

Case study 1 Farming

Farming is one of the most important industries in Northern Ireland. It does not employ many people but it earns a lot of money for the country (£1.9 billion) and provides us with much of the food we eat. Food processing also provides jobs, as does the transport industry, which has to move the products round the country. Land in Northern Ireland is mainly used for grazing – see Resource A.

Resource A ▶

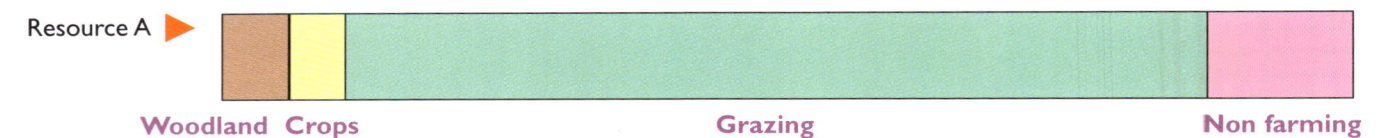

Woodland Crops   Grazing   Non farming

With so much land used for grazing it comes as no surprise to find that dairy cattle, beef cattle and sheep are found on many farms in Northern Ireland. Pigs are also kept on many farms and there are a lot of farms producing chickens and eggs. The two main crops are barley and potatoes. Horticulture produces mushrooms, apples, vegetables and flowers but these are produced only in small quantities in certain areas. The value of these products is shown in Resource B.

Resource B ▶

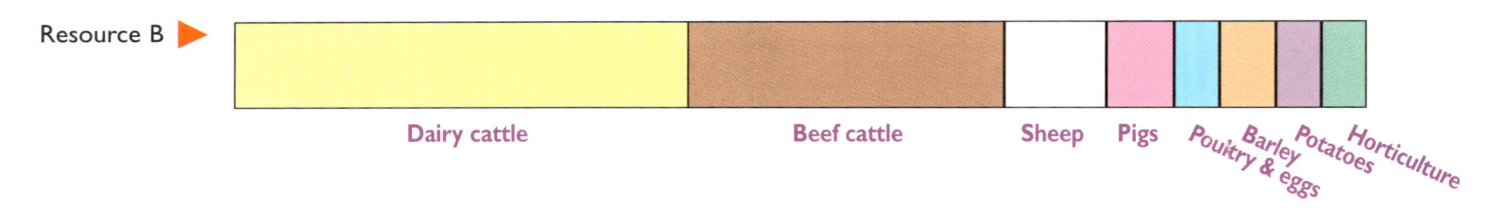

Dairy cattle   Beef cattle   Sheep   Pigs   Poultry & eggs   Barley   Potatoes   Horticulture

Resource C ▼

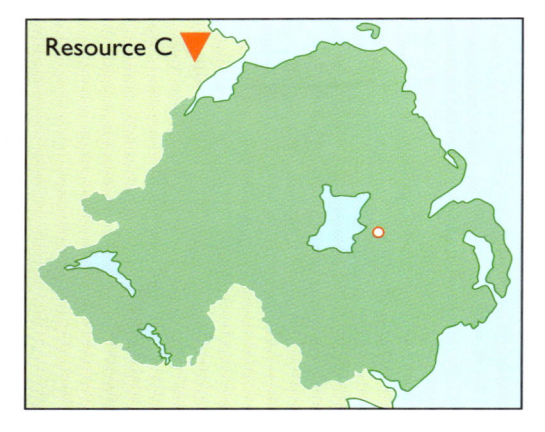

A farm study

We are going to look at a farm 4km south-west of Glenavy, County Antrim (see Resource C). The farm is owned by Mr Wilson and is a cereal/livestock farm. Like most farmers, Mr Wilson concentrates on one or two products. In the 1950s most farmers produced a wider range of crops and animals on smaller farms. All farms in Northern Ireland are commercial farms – they produce their crops and animals for sale, and they use the money raised to buy the goods they need. Resource D shows four questions a farmer has to ask before deciding what he is going to grow on his farm, and the answers Mr Wilson gives for his farm.

Resource D ▼

Questions

Soil What is the soil? light/heavy/loam/fertile	**Climate** What is the climate? rain/temperature/ wind/frost
Relief What is the land like? low/high/flat/steep	**Market** Where will I sell my goods? NI/UK/Europe?

Mr Wilson's answers

Soil light clay with some loam	**Climate** mild summers, cool winters, rain all year
Relief 50m but undulating – going gently up and down	**Market** 1.6m people in NI plus exports abroad

Useful Internet sites: www.loughries.demon.co.uk
www.nfu.org.uk/education/farmstud.shtml

Economic activity

Enkeymore Farm

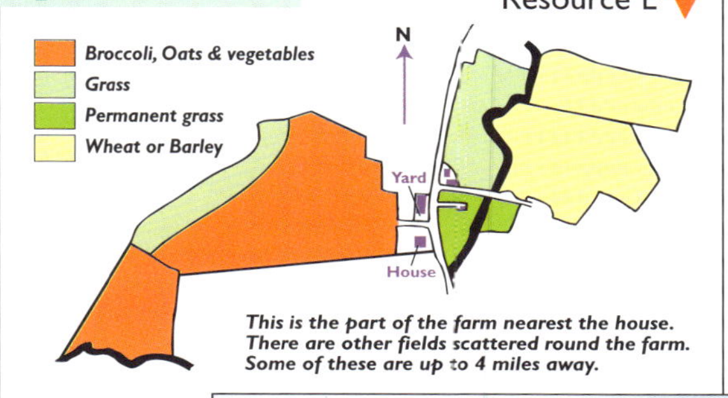

The farm is 184 hectares (ha) in area, made up of 40 ha owned and 144 ha rented. This is a large farm by local standards. The average farm size for Northern Ireland is 36 ha. The GB average is 92 ha while EU farms average only 20 ha. The main products are barley, wheat, oats, oil seed rape, broccoli and beef cattle. The barley, wheat, oats and rape are used for animal feed. They are sold to firms in Lisburn, Ballywalter, Belfast and Randalstown. The broccoli is grown to contract for a large supermarket. The beef cattle are sold to Lurgan Abattoir and supply local butchers and supermarkets. The farmer and his son run the farm, and they either employ two men part time for harvesting and ploughing or contract this out. Many of the jobs are done by machines and this means that less labour is needed. The farm has fourteen machines including five tractors and a combine harvester.

Crops take up most of the land – see Resource E. In order to keep the soil fertile, the farmer practices a four course rotation of barley, barley, oil seed rape, wheat and fertilises each field once or twice a year. Livestock numbers total 70 beef cattle. These are bought in at six months, fattened and sold before they are three years old. Resource F shows a systems diagram for the farm. The **inputs** are what the farmer needs to run his farm. The **processes** show what takes place on the farm. The **outputs** show the main products and their destination.

Resource E

- Broccoli, Oats & vegetables
- Grass
- Permanent grass
- Wheat or Barley

Yard
House

This is the part of the farm nearest the house. There are other fields scattered round the farm. Some of these are up to 4 miles away.

Inputs
- Water
- Power
- Labour ?? men
- ?? machines
- Seed
- Fertiliser

Processes
- Ploughing
- Sowing
- Spraying
- Fattening
- Fertilising
- Harvesting
- Feeding

Outputs
- Animal feed to ??
- Beef to ??
- Broccoli to ??
- Cattle to ??
- waste

Resource F

Exercises

Copy and complete the systems diagram using the information about the farm.

Economic activity

Primary Industry

Case study 2   Quarrying

Northern Ireland has no large-scale mining industry, but it does have a large number of quarries. These provide stone for the construction industry and they are found in all areas of Northern Ireland. Quarrying employs nearly 2000 people in over 160 quarries and provides raw materials for the building industry and road construction.

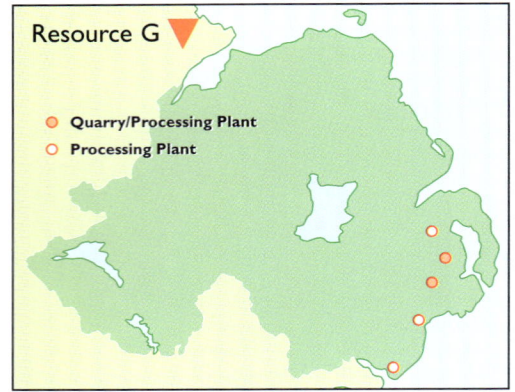

Resource G

○ Quarry/Processing Plant
○ Processing Plant

A study of a quarry

C E Stevenson is a Northern Ireland firm, which operates two quarries and five processing plants in County Down (see Resource G). The quarries mine greywacke, a sedimentary rock, which is quite hard. Resource C on page 20 shows where the rock is found in Northern Ireland. The firm employs over 65 people in the quarries, processing plants and delivery business. The rock is blasted, crushed, and graded by size at the two quarries. The firm makes extensive use of modern machinery and the crushing and grading is fully automated. There are two possible uses for the rock. Firstly it can be sold by the tonne to be used as road fill, hard core or sub-floors for new houses. Secondly it can be processed into concrete products such as breeze-blocks, bricks and ready mix concrete. Stevenson's five processing plants turn out over 56000 breeze-blocks per day as well as 1000 cubic metres of ready mix concrete per week. The main processing plant between Saintfield and Crossgar produces 20000 blocks per day using only 2-3 men. The weighing, mixing and moulding are fully automated and need the minimum labour. All the outputs produced by Stevenson's quarries are used locally in the building and construction industry. Resource H shows a systems diagram of the quarry. Like the farm, it shows the inputs needed to run the business, the processes which take place and the outputs and where they go. The business is unusual in that both primary and secondary industries are found on the same site.

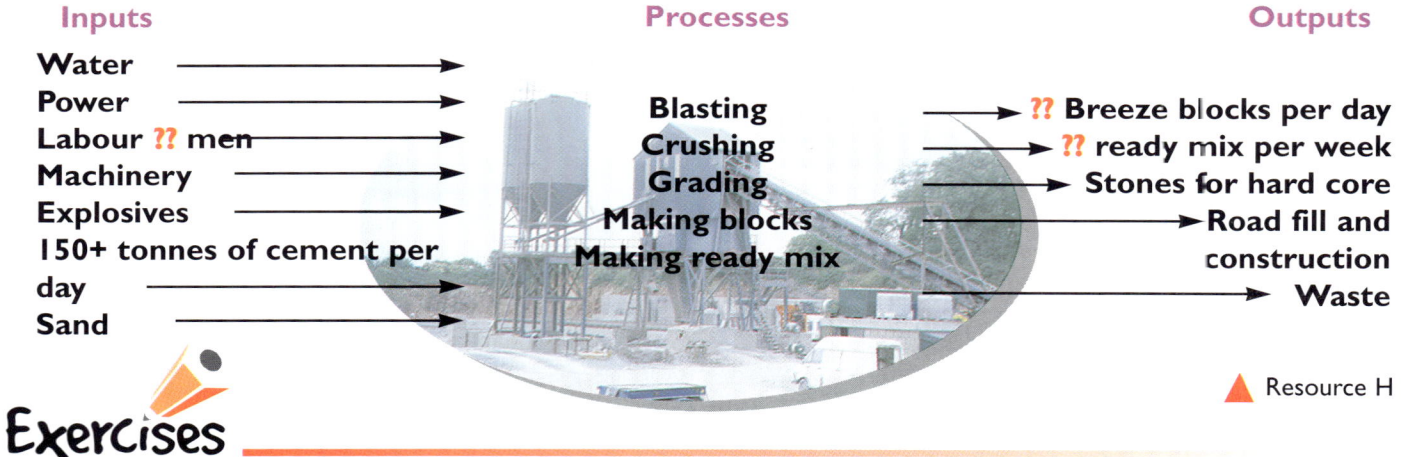

Inputs
- Water
- Power
- Labour ?? men
- Machinery
- Explosives
- 150+ tonnes of cement per day
- Sand

Processes
- Blasting
- Crushing
- Grading
- Making blocks
- Making ready mix

Outputs
- ?? Breeze blocks per day
- ?? ready mix per week
- Stones for hard core
- Road fill and construction
- Waste

▲ Resource H

Exercises

1. Copy and complete the systems diagram using the information about the quarry.
2. People living nearby might object to the quarry. Could you think of three reasons why they might object?
3. What might their reaction be if it was proposed to extend the quarry and make it bigger?
4. If quarries were closed or refused permission to extend, where would the construction industry find the raw materials it needed?
5. Can you think of any other business that would have the primary and secondary activities on the same site?

Economic activity

Secondary Industry

Case study 3 Manufacturing Industry

These industries provide over 80000 jobs. They take resources and raw materials and make them into something useful. They may take their raw materials from other secondary industries, or they may be part of a chain which passes on their product to another industry where it is used as part of a bigger product. Northern Ireland's top ten firms include both secondary (S) and tertiary (T) industries (see Resource I), but bear in mind that in total farming employs nearly 60000 people and is bigger than all of these top ten firms put together.

Resource I

No	Activity	Firm	Product	Employs
1	S	Bombardier/Shorts	aeroplane components	5900
2	T	Tesco	food retailer	5300
3	T	Post Office	shops, letters etc.	4000
4	T	Dunne's Stores	food, clothing retailer	3500
5	T	Safeway	food retailer	2200
6	T	NI Transport Holding Co	buses and trains	3600
7	S	Desmond & Sons	clothing	3400
8	S	Moy Park	processed poultry	2800
9	T	Supervalu	food retailer	2000
10	T/S	Mivan	construction	2500

Source Belfast Telegraph, February 1999

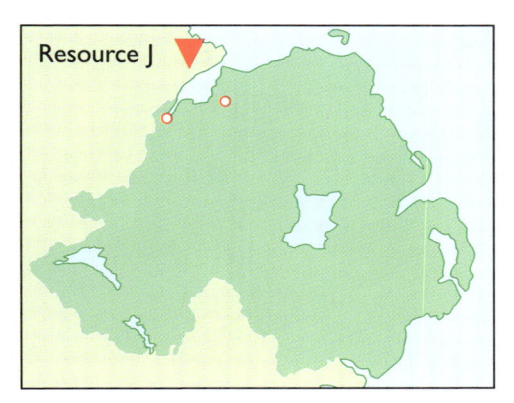

Resource J

A study of Seagate

Seagate is an American **multi-national** which makes disk drives for computers. It has two factories in Northern Ireland at Derry and Limavady (see Resource J). It also has plants in the USA, Singapore, China, Indonesia, Malaysia, Mexico, and Thailand. The Limavady factory imports disk substrates which it buys on the open market. Disk substrates are small disks like a mini CD which are made from nickel plated aluminium. They are the core material on which computer disk drives read, write and store information. In Limavady these go through different processes (cutting, grinding, plating, polishing, and testing) and are then exported to a Seagate factory in Singapore where the magnetic layer is added. They are then sent to another factory to be assembled into disk drives for computers. The computers are finally assembled in another factory, usually in the Far East. The factory runs for 24 hours per day, 365 days per year and the output is 125000 substrates per day. The factory employs around 1000 people out of a Seagate total of 83000. Seagate has a website at: www.seagate.com

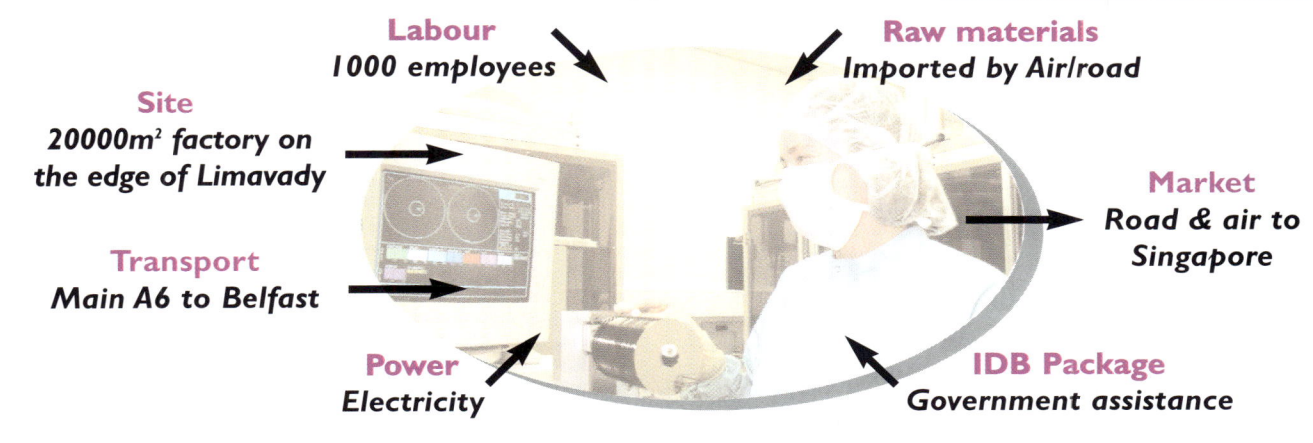

Site
20000m² factory on the edge of Limavady

Labour
1000 employees

Raw materials
Imported by Air/road

Transport
Main A6 to Belfast

Market
Road & air to Singapore

Power
Electricity

IDB Package
Government assistance

Economic activity

Resource L ▼

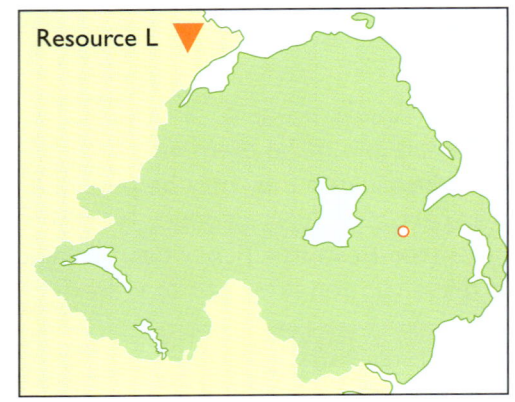

A Study of Montupet

Montupet is a French owned firm, which is located on the outskirts of south west Belfast in the factory once used to produce DeLorean sports cars (see Resource L). It makes car components for major car manufacturers. Montupet is a multi-national company, which has factories in France, Spain, Canada and Mexico. The Belfast factory produces cylinder heads for Ford engines and wheels for Renault, Citroen, Ford and Peugeot cars. They are both made from aluminium, which is smelted and cast in Belfast. Industries choose a location for their factory depending on the seven factors shown in Resource M.

The firm uses sixty five tonnes of aluminium per day (worth £65000). Every day it produces 3400 cylinder heads for various Ford cars and 3000 wheels. The cylinder heads and wheels go through slightly different processes. Resource N shows the main processes for the wheels. (*Desprue* is the process by which the centre is drilled out.) The finished products are transported from Belfast to the UK or France where they are used as **components** in car assembly plants.

Montupet is part of a chain of secondary industries. The first link is the aluminium smelter which smelts the aluminium from the bauxite (aluminium ore). Montupet come next in the chain and they produce parts from aluminium. The final link in the chain is the car assembly plant, which assembles cars from 20000 components manufactured in over 100 factories. Montupet is just one of these component suppliers. They have a website at:

www.montupetuk.co.uk/

Resource M ▼

Labour
750 employees

Site
50000m² factory on a 29 ha site

Transport
Close to M1, easy access to ports

Power
Electricity & 2 gas fired smelters

Raw materials
Imported by road through Larne & Belfast

Market
Renault, Citroen, Ford & Peugeot car assembly plants

IDB Package
Government assistance

Exercises

Draw a systems diagram for either Montupet or Seagate using the information on pages 69-71.

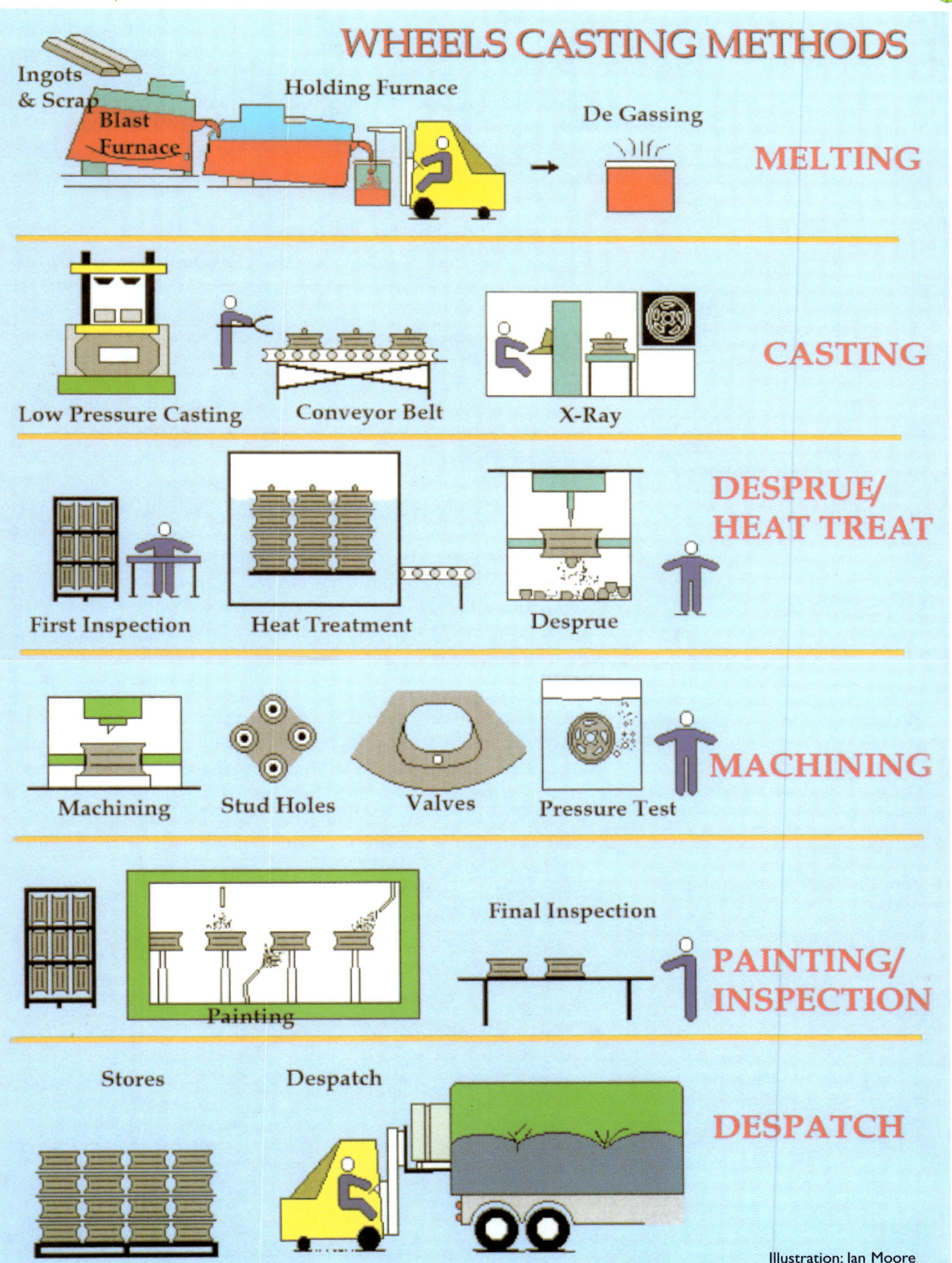

Resource N

Economic activity

WHEELS CASTING METHODS

MELTING
- Ingots & Scrap
- Blast Furnace
- Holding Furnace
- De Gassing

CASTING
- Low Pressure Casting
- Conveyor Belt
- X-Ray

DESPRUE/ HEAT TREAT
- First Inspection
- Heat Treatment
- Desprue

MACHINING
- Machining
- Stud Holes
- Valves
- Pressure Test

PAINTING/ INSPECTION
- Painting
- Final Inspection

DESPATCH
- Stores
- Despatch

Illustration: Ian Moore

Economic activity

Secondary Industry

Case study 4 Food processing

Farming is a very important part of the Northern Ireland economy. It provides the raw materials for a lot of other industries, which take the products and make them into something useful. There are over 300 food processing firms and they provide employment for nearly 20000 people. These firms include dairies processing milk into butter and cheese, feed mills using barley for animal food and meat plants changing pork into bacon and sausages.

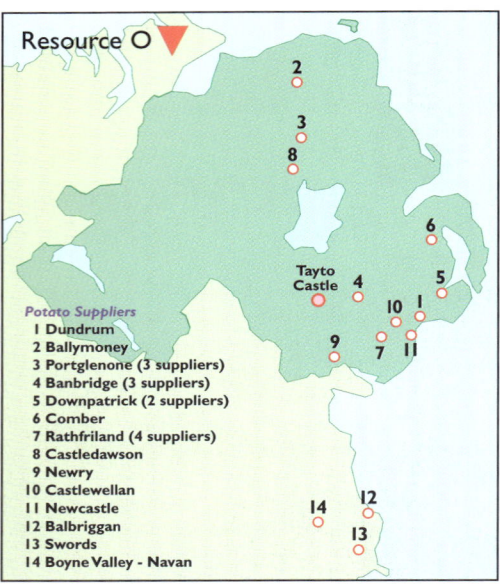

A study of Tayto Crisps

We are going to look at Tayto Castle in Tandragee, County Armagh. (See Resource O). Tayto began production in 1956 with six workers. The new factory was built in 1979 and since then over £20 million has been invested in replacing and updating equipment. The factory now employs over 300 people making a wide range of crisps and snacks. Like other industries, the factory has inputs, processes and outputs (see Resource P). The main input is potatoes (13500 tonnes per year) which are grown to contract by over 20 farmers in Northern Ireland and the Republic. The company also uses 3000 litres of sunflower oil per day, imported from overseas (Brazil, Portugal or Spain). A firm in Warrenpoint makes the boxes, while the packaging is imported from a firm in Dublin. The processes are more complicated than you would think. After harvesting, the potatoes have to be stored. From the months of July through to October the potatoes are harvested and transported to the factory where they are placed in storage and are used through the incoming year for the production of the crisps. When they are needed, they have to be cleaned and peeled; then they go through the processes outlined in the box below.

Resource O

Potato Suppliers
1 Dundrum
2 Ballymoney
3 Portglenone (3 suppliers)
4 Banbridge (3 suppliers)
5 Downpatrick (2 suppliers)
6 Comber
7 Rathfriland (4 suppliers)
8 Castledawson
9 Newry
10 Castlewellan
11 Newcastle
12 Balbriggan
13 Swords
14 Boyne Valley - Navan

1. They are sliced into 1.2mm slices.
2. Washed to remove the starch.
3. Blanched (partly cooked) for one to three minutes.
4. Dried to remove surface water.
5. Fried for two minutes at 170C.
6. Dried.
7. Flavoured.
8. Weighed and packed in bags and then boxes.
9. Stored and transported to customer.

The main outputs are crisps and corn snacks, over 90% of which are sold within Northern Ireland. The factory also sells waste potatoes, skins and crisps to local farmers. It recycles its heat from the fryers to heat the offices. The oil is sold on to firms that can use it, and excess starch, which is removed at stage two, is sold to the paper and glue industry. If you want to see all this for yourselves, you can visit the factory by telephoning 028 38 840249. Tours are conducted at 10.30 and 1.30 Monday to Thursday and 10.30 only on Friday. The factory is not open in the evening, on public holidays or at weekends. You will have a chance of eating some of the one million bags of crisps and corn snacks they produce every day. Tayto have a website at: www.tayto.com

Resource P

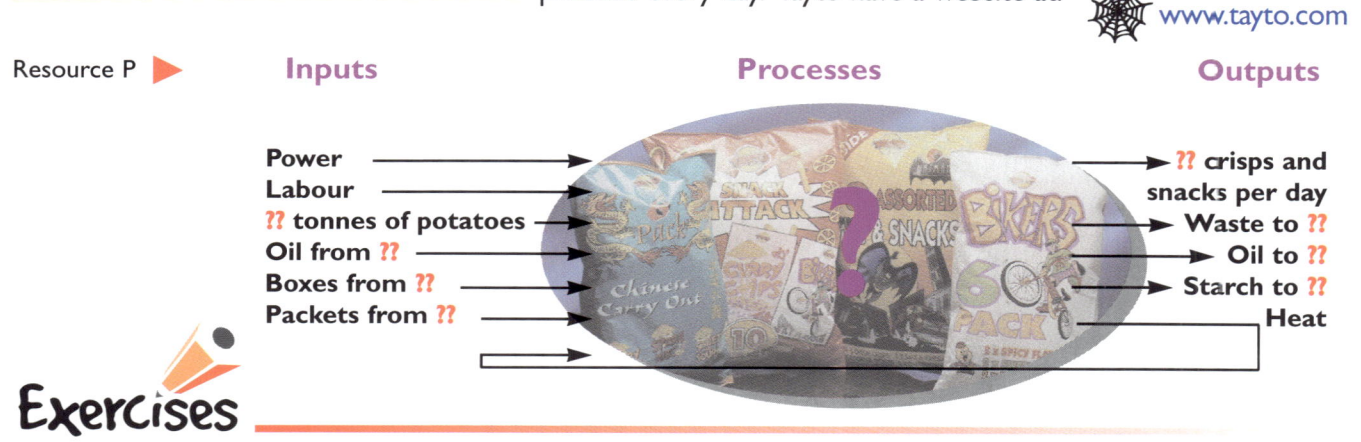

Inputs
- Power
- Labour
- ?? tonnes of potatoes
- Oil from ??
- Boxes from ??
- Packets from ??

Processes

Outputs
- ?? crisps and snacks per day
- Waste to ??
- Oil to ??
- Starch to ??
- Heat

Exercises

Copy and complete the systems diagram illustrated.

Economic activity

Scenes from Tayto Castle

Economic activity

Tertiary Industry

Case study 5 A Supermarket

Supermarkets are an important part of the retail distribution trade, which employs over 60000 people in Northern Ireland. These range from the large supermarkets like Tesco, with nearly 40 outlets and 5300 jobs, to the local garage/corner shop with three or four part-time jobs. The industries also support over 20000 jobs in transport, as goods are shipped into Northern Ireland through the main ports, and are then distributed around the country in containers and lorries. There are a number of large supermarket chains in Northern Ireland – Tesco, Dunnes, Safeway, Supervalu, Co-op, Sainsbury's and Marks & Spencer. Five of these are UK based and two are based in Ireland. The large supermarkets often locate their stores in out of town shopping centres. These may consist of one large store and/or a collection of shops and other service outlets with a car parking facility, located near a major road or junction, which are easily accessible to large numbers of people.

Resource Q ▼

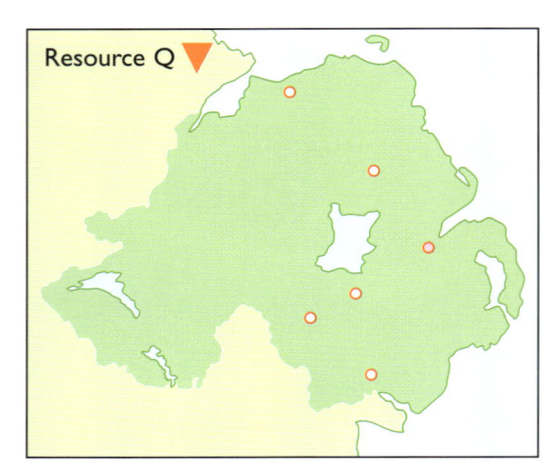

Sainsbury's at Forestside

This is just one of six Sainsbury's stores in Northern Ireland (Resource Q). The store is located on the outskirts of Belfast, on the former Supermac centre site which was one of the most successful supermarkets in Northern Ireland. Sainsbury's acquired the site in 1995 and renamed it Forestside. Sainsbury's built its brand new store, the first phase of the property development, which was timed to begin trading in spring 1997 when the Supermac store closed. Resource R shows the main factors, which have made this a successful shopping centre.

Resource R ▼

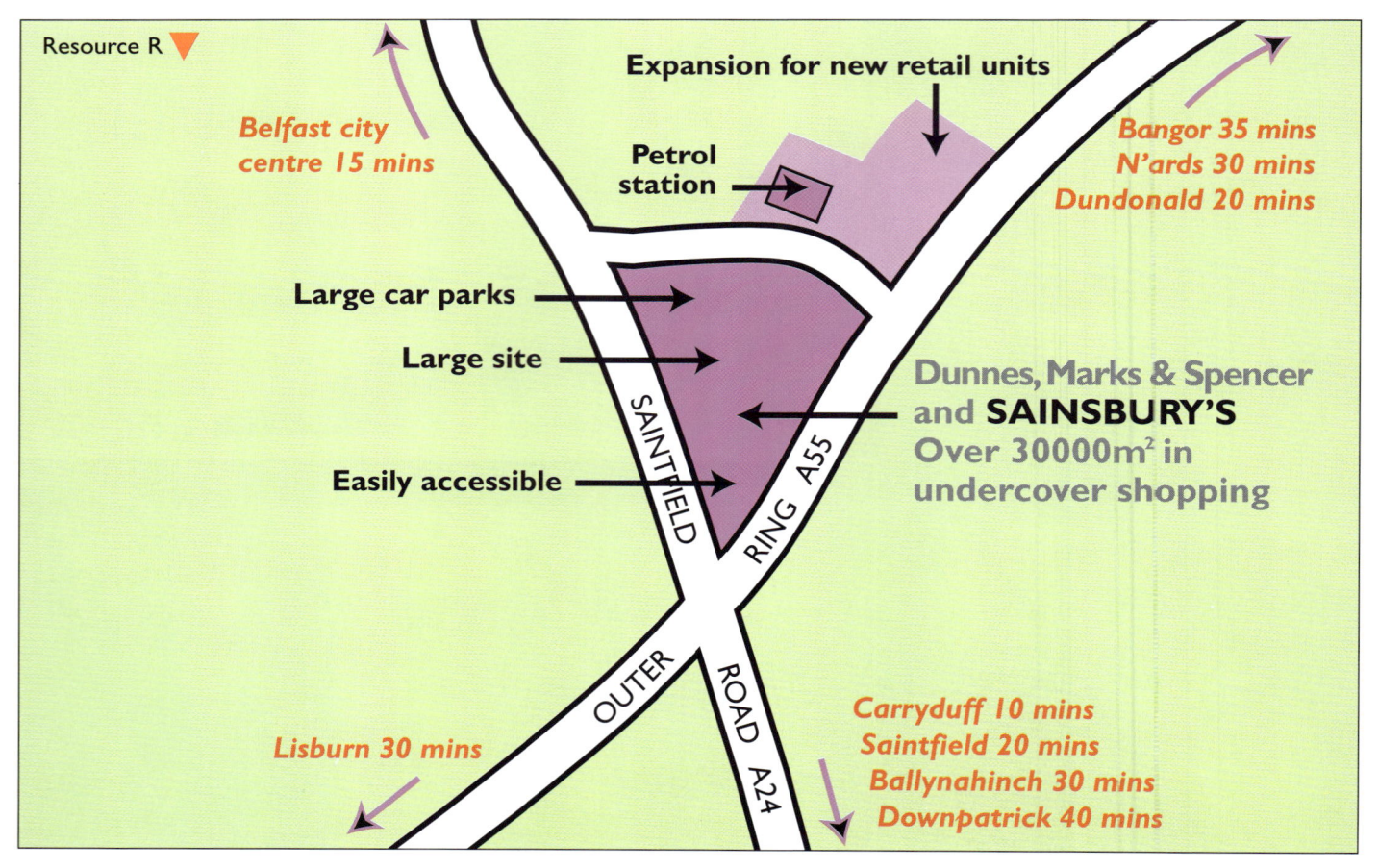

- Expansion for new retail units
- Petrol station
- Belfast city centre 15 mins
- Bangor 35 mins / N'ards 30 mins / Dundonald 20 mins
- Large car parks
- Large site
- Easily accessible
- Dunnes, Marks & Spencer and **SAINSBURY'S** Over 30000m² in undercover shopping
- SAINTFIELD
- RING A55
- OUTER ROAD A24
- Lisburn 30 mins
- Carryduff 10 mins / Saintfield 20 mins / Ballynahinch 30 mins / Downpatrick 40 mins

Sketch of Forestside

Economic activity

The store employs 720 people out of a total NI workforce of 2000. On average there are 48000 customers per week who use 90000 plastic bags at the 42 checkouts. The goods are brought in by lorry, and around 90 lorries make deliveries every week. The prices are bar coded and the whole stock system is computerised. The manager can tell not only how many bags of crisps have been sold in a week, but which brand and flavour. Orders can then be submitted for the following week. Popular items have extra orders placed, while items that do not sell well can be discontinued. Sainsbury's try to use local suppliers and over 80 local firms supply goods to the store. Sainsbury's Forestside was the first NI supermarket to open 24 hours Friday to Saturday in August 1997. This was so successful the store now operates 24 hour opening Monday to Saturday, including the Sainsbury's petrol station. Forestside is the only Sainsbury's store in the group, outside London, to do this. A successful store attracts more customers from other stores and they will have to offer similar facilities to keep their customers happy.

A successful store acts as a magnet for other shops and retail outlets. These in turn draw in more customers and attract further businesses. Phase two of the property development at Forestside opened in autumn 1998 and the centre added a large Marks & Spencer and a Dunnes store. There are a further 32 shops and most of these are high order shops selling comparison goods like clothes. Customers can buy their convenience goods in Sainsbury's, they may have a snack and then walk around the other shops to look at comparison goods.

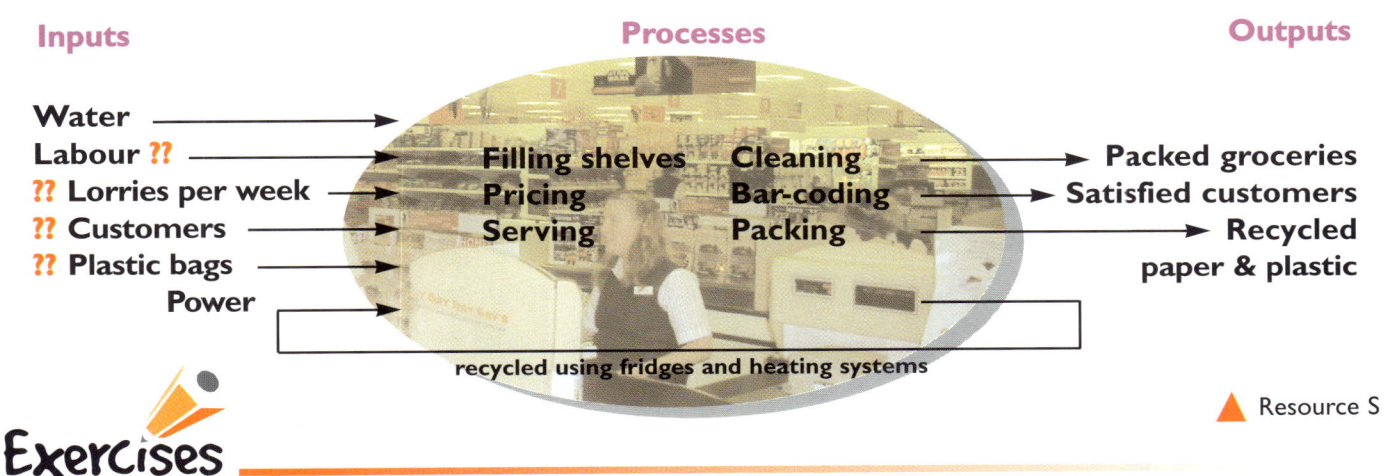

www.sainsburys.co.uk

Inputs
- Water
- Labour ??
- ?? Lorries per week
- ?? Customers
- ?? Plastic bags
- Power

Processes
- Filling shelves
- Pricing
- Serving
- Cleaning
- Bar-coding
- Packing

recycled using fridges and heating systems

Outputs
- Packed groceries
- Satisfied customers
- Recycled paper & plastic

▲ Resource S

Exercises

Copy and complete the systems diagram in Resource S.

Economic activity

Tertiary Industry

Case study 6 Tourism

Tourism is an important part of the Northern Ireland economy. In 1998, nearly 1.5 million tourists brought in £217 million to the Northern Ireland economy. Local people who took their holiday in Northern Ireland spent another £63 million. On average each tourist spent £147 on accommodation, food, travel and entertainment.

What exactly is a *tourist*? A tourist is a visitor to the country who stays at least twenty-four hours in the country visited. They can be divided into three types, holidaymakers, business people and those visiting friends and relatives (VFR).

The main visitor attractions in Northern Ireland are:

Resource T shows where these visitors come from.

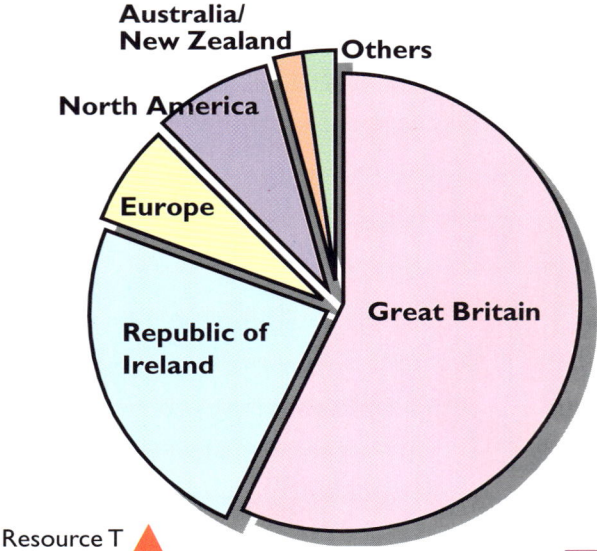

Northern Ireland Tourist Board

Top 10 Visitor attractions

1. Giant's Causeway Visitor Centre
2. Pickie Family Fun Park (Bangor)
3. Ulster Museum
4. Belfast Zoo
5. Belleek Pottery
6. Ulster Folk & Transport Museum
7. Oxford Island Nature Reserve
8. Murlough Nature Reserve
9. Exploris (Portaferry)
10. Ulster American Folk Park (Omagh)

Resource T — pie chart: Great Britain, Republic of Ireland, Europe, North America, Australia/New Zealand, Others

Resource U shows why these people visit Northern Ireland.

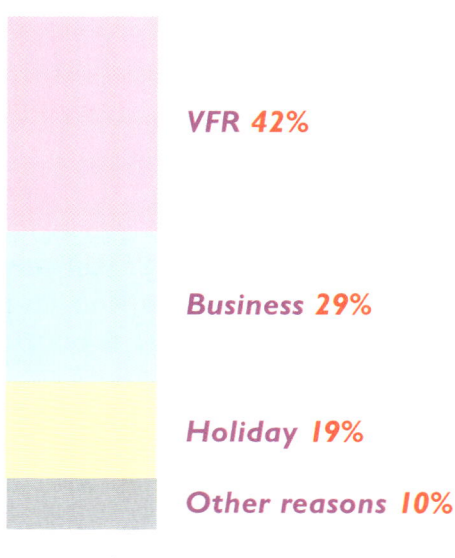

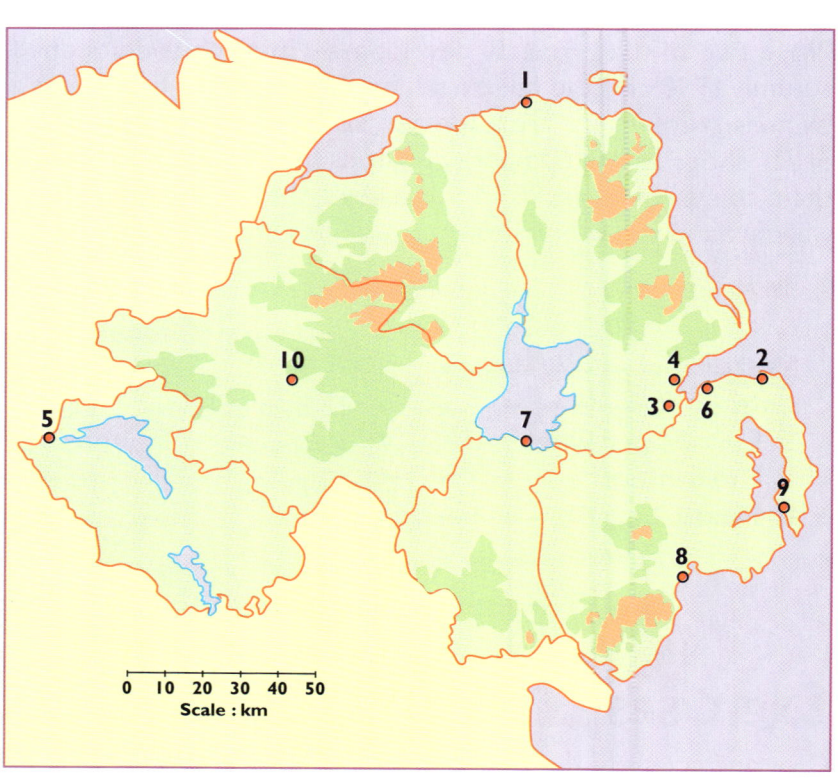

- VFR 42%
- Business 29%
- Holiday 19%
- Other reasons 10%

Resource U

Scale: 0 10 20 30 40 50 km

Economic activity

Tourism is important in all areas of Northern Ireland. One example is along the North Coast in an area stretching from Magilligan Strand in the west to Fair Head in the east. The Giant's Causeway Visitor Centre alone recorded over 400,000 visits in 1998. It is reasonable to assume that these visitors went to other sites along the North Coast and spent money in hotels, restaurants, shops and cafés. If they came from outside Northern Ireland then they may also have visited other areas of the country and spent money. The local economy benefits directly from the jobs and money that tourists bring. It also benefits indirectly from the improved facilities and **infrastructure** that are provided to attract tourists.

Sometimes tourism can have drawbacks. It can be argued that, occasionally, pressure is put on the natural environment, for example increased traffic on local roads. Also, jobs tend to be seasonal, running only from April to September.

Part of the North Coast area is shown on the map extract on page 8.

Top: The Giant's Causeway. *Bottom:* Pickie Family Fun Park

www.ni-tourism.com
www.nitb.com
www.ulst.ac.uk/nitourism

Exercises

Using the map on page 8:

1) List any primary or secondary jobs that you can identify.
2) Find at least six features that provide evidence that tourism is important in the area.
3) List the tertiary jobs that are created by tourists in the area.
4) What could the Government, Tourist Board or the Councils do to increase the number of tourists?
5) Resource V shows the number of visitors over the last nine years. Can you think of any reasons which would explain the drop in visitors in 1996 and 1997?
6) List at least three ways that an increase in tourism might have a bad effect on the local area and its environment.

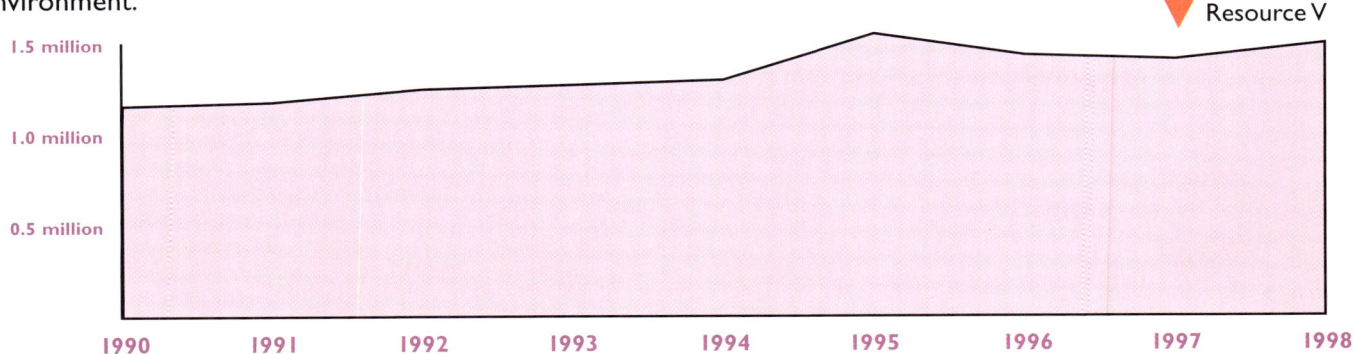

▼ Resource V

Using the Internet

Most schools are either already "online" or soon will be. Access to the Internet puts literally thousands of up to date resources at your fingertips. Many statistics can be updated by using Government websites and most firms and organisations have sites where you can find figures that can be used in lessons and projects. Many of these sites are mentioned in the relevant pages in the book, while others are ring sites or lists of good sites which have been checked and found to be useful.

The following addresses that were correct and "online" in July 1999 are either educational sites or general sites that give a list of useful addresses. Once you find the site you can then follow different links according to the data you want to find. Some of the addresses elsewhere in the book will be duplicated here or found as you go through. The idea is to get you started with sites that have been found to be useful, and then you can explore from these. Good hunting!

The BBC has a very good schools website with a lot of information. They also have an Education Webguide to a wide range of subjects including Geography. Go to http://bbc.co.uk/education-webguide/pkg_main.p_home then follow the links through to the Geography section.

The Northern Ireland Network for Education also has a site that is a good jumping off point for other sites. It can be found www.nine.org.uk . Click on Key Stage 3 – 4, and then click on Geography. This site is provided by Dr Bill MacAfee at the NUU and is a most useful site if you are unfamiliar with the Internet. As well as giving links to other sites it gives you a beginners guide to using the net and has a section on using search engines to find geographical information.

Another general site with excellent content and links is found at Geography World. The address is http://members.aol.com/bowermanb/101.html . This is an American site but it is worth a visit if only to see the daylight map which shows where the sun is shining. Try the climate and weather section!

There are two Government sites that are useful to the geographer. The first is the UK site at www.ons.gov.uk/ons_f.htm and the second is the Northern Ireland version at www.nics.gov.uk . These sometimes charge for the information you want, so be warned.

Channel 4 has a schools site at http://schools.channel4.con/home_001.cfm . Another school site is at www.schoolzone.co.uk, then click on surf schoolzone, then Geography.

Finally there is a ring site at www.webring.org/cgi-bin/webring?ring=geography;list .

Once you have found a useful site it can be stored in your favourites section or bookmarked so as you don't have to type the address in every time you want to use it.

Glossary and Index

A **Anticyclone** — An area of high pressure which brings settled weather. *40*

Atlas — A book of maps. *4*

B **Birth rate** — The number of babies born per thousand people per year. *59-61*

Bridging point — A place where it is easy to cross a river. *51-52*

C **Climate** — The pattern of weather over a year, taken from 30 year averages. *13, 32-37*

Commercial — Land used mainly for shops and offices. *44, 50*

Comparison goods — Expensive goods which are compared with others before they are bought eg furniture, cars, dishwasher. *48, 75*

Component — A small part of a bigger product such as wheels for a car. *69-70*

Convenience goods — Inexpensive goods which are bought regularly and without a lot of thought eg bread, milk, sweets and newspapers. *48, 75*

Core — The centre of the Earth. *18*

Crust — The shell around the Earth, composed of rocks. *18, 21*

D **Death rate** — The number of people dying per thousand people per year. *59-61*

Defensive site — A site which is easy to defend, such as a hilltop or island. *51-52*

Densely populated — An area where many people live. *54-57*

Dependent population — The part of the population which depends on others for their support, usually under 15 and over 60. *63*

Depression — An area of low pressure which usually brings cloud, wind and rain. *38-41*

E **Economically active** — The part of the population which is of working age, usually 15 – 59. *63*

Ecosystem — A community and its environment working together. *13-17*

Elements of weather — Parts of weather that can be measured eg rain, temperature, and wind speed. *30*

Environment — The conditions in which an organism lives. *16*

Erosion — The wearing away of rock by sea, rivers, wind or ice. *22-29*

F **Food chain** — A series of organisms each dependent on the next for food. *14*

Fossils — The remains of animals and plants preserved in rock. *19, 20*

G **Growth rate** — The increase in the population per thousand, worked out by subtracting the death rate from the birth rate. *59-60*

H **Habitat** — The environment in which an organism lives. *15*

Hierarchy — Settlements put in order according to their size. *45, 48, 53*

High order shops — Shops which sell comparison goods, they are bought less frequently, and cost more money. *48-49*

Horizon — The layers in a soil profile. *17*

I **IDB** — Industrial Development Board, a government organisation which encourages and helps industries that want to set up in Northern Ireland. *69, 70*

Igneous — "Fire-made" rock formed by cooling magma. *21*

Industrial — Land used mainly for factories and industry. *44, 50*

Infrastructure — The services provided for the area e.g. roads, electricity, sewage, water, telephones. *77*

L **LEDC** — Less economically developed country – a poorer country. *60*

Low order shops — Shops whose goods are bought more frequently and cost less money. *48-49*

M	**MEDC**	More economically developed country – a richer country. **60**
	Mantle	A zone of molten rock between the core and the crust of the Earth. **18, 21**
	Meander	A large bend or loop in a river. **26**
	Metamorphic	"Changed" rocks which heat and/or pressure have altered. **21**
	Meteorologist	A person who studies the weather. **30-31**
	Migration	Movement of people from one area/country to another. **59-61**
	Multi-national	A company with factories in more than one country. **69-70**
N	**Non-renewable**	Resources which cannot be replaced once they run out, like coal or oil. **20**
P	**Polar front**	The line dividing warm and cold air along which depressions travel. **38**
	Population density	The average number of people per square km who live in an area. **56-58**
	Population pyramid	A diagram which shows the breakdown of the population by age and sex. **62**
	Port	A settlement where ships can load and unload goods. **51-52**
	Primary activity	Jobs which obtain the raw materials or resources which we need. **64-68**
R	**Recreational**	Land used mainly for leisure and recreation. **44**
	Residential	Land used mainly for housing. **44**
	Resource	Something obtained from the Earth, which can be used by man. **20**
	Renewable	Resources which renew themselves over and over again, like trees or fish. **20**
	Route centre	A settlement which grows up where important roads meet. **51-52**
	Rural	In the countryside. **42-43, 55**
S	**Seasonal jobs**	Jobs that only last for part of the year e.g. waiter in a resort hotel. **77**
	Secondary activity	Jobs which take the raw material and make it into something useful. **64-65, 69-73**
	Sedimentary	"Layered" rocks laid down in layers under the sea. **21, 68**
	Settlement	A place where people live. **42-53**
	Site	The actual place where a settlement grows up. **42-43, 51-52**
	Soil	A mixture of weathered rock, humus and minerals, which forms the top few metres of the Earth's crust. **13-17**
	Soil profile	A slice cut down into the ground to expose the soil. **17**
	Sparsely populated	An area where very few people live. **54-57**
T	**Tertiary activity**	Jobs which provide a service for other people. **64, 74-77**
	Temperate	Moderate, without extremes. **32, 36**
	Tourist	A visitor to a country who stays at least 24 hours in the country visited. **76-77**
U	**Urban**	In villages, towns or cities. **42-43, 50**
W	**Weather**	The day to day changes in the air around us. **30-41**
	Weathering	The breakdown of rock by weather, plants, and animals. **22**

A note on geographical terminology

Great Britain is made up of England, Scotland and Wales.
The **United Kingdom** is made up of Great Britain and Northern Ireland.
The term **British Isles** is used in its geographical sense to mean Great Britain, the island of Ireland and the smaller islands adjacent to both. It is not used in any political sense.